BUILDING YOUR CHILD'S FAITH

In appreciation for your support of Focus on the Family, please accept this copy of *Building Your Child's Faith* by Alice Chapin. Your contributions enable this organization to address the needs of homes through radio, television, literature and counseling.

We trust that the suggestions found on the following pages will help you develop your child's relationship with Christ. We're confident that this book will make a fine addition to your family's bookshelf.

Focus on the Family
P.O. Box 500
Arcadia, CA 91006

BUILDING YOUR CHILD'S FAITH

by

Alice Chapin

CAMPUS CRUSADE FOR CHRIST

HERE'S LIFE PUBLISHERS, INC.
San Bernardino, California
92402

BUILDING YOUR CHILD'S FAITH
by Alice Chapin

A Campus Crusade for Christ book
Published by
HERE'S LIFE PUBLISHERS, INC.
P. O. Box 1576
San Bernardino, CA 92402

ISBN 0-86605-115-5
Library of Congress Catalog Card 83-072437
HLP Product No. 403204
© 1983,Here's Life Publishers, Inc.

Manufactured in the United States of America

Unless otherwise indicated, all Scripture quotations are
from the New American Standard Bible, © The Lockman
Foundation 1960, 1962, 1963, 1968, 1971, 1972, 1975,
and are used by permission.

CONTENTS

INTRODUCTION

Poverty-stricken children are not just those whose parents are very poor. Children who are undernourished spiritually are also impoverished. Having little Bible knowledge or none at all, they do not know how to live with power or how to die with dignity and confidence.

Responsibility for teaching children about God is not transferable. It belongs squarely with parents by divine decree and they have only about 20 years or less to fulfill this responsibility. There is no second chance at the job. Realizing the urgency for success in child-rearing, I collected ideas for this book from many women in seminars I taught on "How to Share Your Faith With Your Children." I believe you can succeed as a parent or guardian with or without a great knowledge of Scripture, a college or high school diploma or a gift for speaking eloquently.

Parents can deliver the doctrine a child needs at handy times, in just the right sized doses, while holding parent-child conversations, rocking, doing dishes together, playing on the floor, smelling flowers, hiking, sitting around the dinner table, getting ready for bed or during planned times. This style of teaching can help to ensure that later, as an adult, the child will not be confused. He will not struggle with the basics of the faith because he will have mastered them and found them workable long before the pressures of adult life close in.

Where is stability in life? The average family picks up and moves about once every four years. Parents and grandparents die. Teachers retire, and schools are bulldozed away to make room for new structures. Our kids need security. They need to be able to count on at least one unchanging constant in life. That has been provided: It is God. But a child does not have built-in spiritual knowledge or intuition. He needs to be taught about his heavenly Father.

On a plane to Florida I chatted with an aerospace engineer whose college-age son had recently found his way into the "Jesus movement." This brilliant man confided in me, "I am worried about Kim because I don't know whether he has gotten into something harmless and transitory or into something dangerous, or into something kooky or wonderful. I don't have enough spiritual know-how to determine that. Worse, Kim is asking me to read the Bible and follow Christ too. He says he has found peace he never had before. I don't even think religion is necessary. Look how far I have come without it! I earn $50,000 a year, own a $90,000 home with built-in pool and tennis courts, belong to the most exclusive country club in the county, and have famous friends in Washington, D.C. Besides all that, I am well-respected, and not a bad guy.''

''Where do you go for help when you are sick or in trouble?'' I asked.

''Well, last year I did have a bad heart attack,'' he answered. ''It scared the dickens out of me, but I depended on my wife, the wisdom of the top heart specialist in the country and then on a private nurse.'' He paused a moment. ''My wife died 6 months ago.''

I continued, ''Doctors are not infallible, nor do they live forever. Suppose yours had been killed in a car accident and the nurse had been kept home by sickness when you needed her. Or suppose you had been taken ill on the lonely Appalachian Trail, miles away from any human help. Who would you have depended on then?''

There was a long silence. ''I guess I would have had to depend on myself. . . '' His voice trailed off as he looked at me beseechingly.

''But you were very ill. . .'' I reminded him.

He saw my point. This well-educated and independent man had no further answer. He saw quickly the need for some higher person to care about him and comfort him when friends dropped away. Sadly, like so many young people today, he had been brought up in a humanistic society that teaches man is adequate for his own needs.

"Please consider the alternative way of life your son has found," I urged, handing him a small booklet that shows in four steps how to become a Christian. We both agreed that it is sometimes embarrassing for us parents to have our children teach us things about life that we should have taught them. To be instructed by a young son or daughter can be humiliating. Somewhere along the line this very smart man had missed it spiritually and even now in his middle years, seemed defensive and resistant about yielding to Christ because his intellectual and parental ego were threatened. I wondered why this intelligent man's parents had not challenged him in his early life to believe and trust in God. Were his son and I the first to share Christ with him?

There is a vital concept that sound Christianity establishes in children and it is: If God loves me and forgives me, I must be worth something. I must be okay. How much it is needed in this age of inferiority complexes and guilt trips! The child who knows that a caring God accompanies him to school, rides beside him on the school bus and travels with him anywhere he goes on his bicycle, is a child who feels more secure. He senses order and constancy in life. He knows he is loved, and understands that God is a source of help. A parent is responsible to impart this assurance to the child.

Some parents say that they do not want to influence a child's religious beliefs. They will allow him to decide for himself when he grows up, they reason. But this is an irresponsible attitude. After all, these same parents DO choose to be an influence in their youngsters' activities, choice of friends, education, clothing, manners, etc., so why should they shirk the responsibility to influence their child's spiritual beliefs? Are they bending to the will of certain psychologists who consider it best that children be open-minded and think for themselves on issues?

On the wall of one probation officer's counseling room in a Georgia juvenile jail, I read:

> You parents go to all kinds of trouble to see that your kids DON'T learn certain patterns of behavior. Why not expend that much energy on what you DO want them to learn *about God?* Only God changes people. Kids who come in here need changing!

That makes sense. A parent who neglects teaching a boy or girl about God very likely relegates the youngster to a childhood of fear, hate, restlessness and disharmony with himself and others. Fortunately, a child doesn't have to fall into that kind of pattern, because he can be directed in the right way. Kids often have 14-karat faith. They usually believe without questioning and seldom complicate faith with doubt. A young child, almost without exception, who is told about God's love on the cross, accepts it in innocent faith, unmixed with argument. But parents *must* confront children with the Bible and with Christ while they are young, because by adolescence many youngsters are no longer open to spiritual truth, and statistics show the chances of a person turning to Christ as an adult are even smaller.

Even regular Sunday school training does not get the religious education job done. Forty-five minutes a week just is not enough time to develop a working knowledge of the Christian faith. Nor is it sufficient time for producing confident people with high moral standards who have enough biblical brains to know why they are on earth, how to love themselves and others and how to live boldly without being a slave to fear. Furthermore, children who are placed in a church's program of religious education often are not left there because the father's or mother's job necessitates moving. Some children attend Sunday school only sporadically at best because their attendance conforms to the parents' Sunday morning late or early rising habits. For all of these reasons, it *must* be the parents' priority and responsibility to teach children about God. Moms and dads who are depending on the church, the pastor, the Sunday school teacher or fate to get the job done are building on quicksand.

Young people are searching for God. In one survey, 89 percent of the students said they did not know how to become a Christian and 60 percent indicated they were looking for a faith. These statistics come from Campus Crusade for Christ, an organization specializing in presenting the claims of Christ to people under 25. They were gleaned from interviews with 10,500 high school and university students. So it appears that we have become a nation of spiritual illiterates. Although the Bible is the world's best seller, most schools pass it silently by, scared by recent, rather blurred Supreme Court rulings on prayer and Bible in public educational institutions.

It is no wonder young people are so easily led into strange and sometimes awful paths. Witchcraft is on the upswing. Many parents are reported to be paying thousands of dollars to kidnap their own youngsters back from cult groups, which are growing in fantastic numbers. But a child who grows up with a strong biblical knowledge and with a faith that produces helpful resources in times of trouble is not so likely to be enticed by every new religious wind that blows his way. True, some adolescents who have been spiritually well-reared begin to question the faith, and wander away in teen years, but at least they know God is there, and they have a spiritual nest to return to when they feel the need.

Bible-taught people are wise. Those who understand God's Word know how to reject or accept life as it comes along, and controversial subjects such as evolution, abortion, the meaning of life, war and death can be evaluated in definite terms. The Bible is psychologically sound, and the born-again man or woman who has had time to try out the faith, has the best chance of staying out of the psychiatrist's office because that person has immediate access to higher help for the problems that stem from guilt, feelings of inferiority, hate, selfishness, loneliness, fear and incompatability.

The most natural place to teach a child about Christ is at the parent's knee. Mom and Dad have the patience, love and motivation to get the job done best. A child's early training may well determine whether or not he can accept his lot in life contentedly. Indeed, it may determine his belief that there is a God to depend on. The ultimatum to parents to get this job done is clear, and it comes from God Himself:

"And you shall love the Lord your God with all your heart and with all your soul and with all your might.

''And these words, which I am commanding you today, shall be on your heart; and you shall teach them diligently to your sons and shall talk of them when you sit in your house and when you walk by the way and when you lie down and when you rise up'' (Deuteronomy 6:5-7).

Chapter 1

Your Child and the Bible

O God, Thou hast taught me from my youth; And I still declare Thy wondrous deeds.

And even when I am old and gray, O God, do not forsake me, Until I declare Thy strength to this generation, Thy power to all who are to come.

—David, in Psalm 71:17,18

At first glance, the Bible's standards may seem wild and unrealistic, its stories fantastic, its instructions outrageous. No one, children included, can be expected to believe the Bible unless they read it often. Its rules do not follow the natural inclinations of twentieth-century people:

Love your enemy.
Pray for those who misuse you.
Turn the other cheek.

It is better to give than to receive.
You shall not commit adultery.
Love your father and your mother.
If you want to be great, be a servant of the rest.

But daily Bible reading with its constant exposure to God's rules likely will bring understanding, belief in its reasonableness and commitment to its truths. For our leader, Jesus Christ, really did know what He was talking about when He laid out God's blueprint for life.

It is sometimes difficult to lure a child into a book that is twenty centuries old, much less to convince him that anything or anyone could really be the same yesterday, today and forever.

Children have no eagerness to maintain the past. They sense the staggering swiftness of the world's progress. As planes fly 2,000 miles per hour overhead, kindergarteners are mastering basic computer skills. And high technological advances promise much, much more with each passing day.

Nevertheless, it is the inescapable calling of parents to lead their sons and daughters into the Book of books early in life. Today's children must somehow be taught that while the world changes, God does not. They must be led to seek the guidance, instruction and unchanging truth that transcends time and transforms lives. They must see Scripture as a precious heritage preserved just for them.

Which Bible?

There are many choices in an English language Bible. Some versions were first published centuries ago; some are just completed. Some are shirt-pocket size; others are large with oversize print. Some have traditional black covers; others have denim or brightly colored covers. There is even a three-hole punched notebook edition with wide empty margins for personal notes.

But the most important consideration when purchasing a Bible for your child is not size or color but the translation or version you select. If your family attends church and Sunday school regularly, you are probably accustomed to using one version more than others. While the King James Bible is the best known (a 350-year-old translation), some people feel it is too difficult for children to understand.

So other translations have appeared on the market. Although they are easier to understand, scholars differ among themselves as to which is the most accurate. The Revised Standard Version (1952) is not well received among many evangelicals. The New American Standard Bible (1963) is more readily received, and maintains some of the majesty of the King James Version but with updated language. The New International Version (1973) is highly acceptable to evangelicals, employs modern language, and has been hailed as a very reliable translation.

The Living Bible has helped millions of people to unravel Scripture because its language is as up-to-date and modern as any book on the library shelf. Kenneth Taylor, author of the popular edition, makes no claims for extreme accuracy in its finest phrasing, but for the lay reader,. the vital main themes are kept very much intact. It should be noted, however, that the Living Bible is a loose paraphrase and not a translation. That is, it is a restatement or rephrasing of what the Bible means; it is not a word-for-word translation from the ancient languages of Scripture.

But no matter which version you give to your child, the answers to man's problems are likely to remain locked between its covers unless you, as a parent, personally take the responsibility to instruct him or her in the teachings of God's holy Word.

> ''All Scripture is inspired by God and profitable for teaching, for reproof, for correction, for training in righteousness; that the man of God may be adequate, equipped for every good work'' (II Timothy 3:16,17, NASB)

Getting Started

The Bible can make a dynamic difference in any child's life. That is our motivation as parents and teachers. But it takes both ingenuity and creativity to inject biblical brains into our youngsters. And no project ever gets off the ground without a master plan. So first of all . . .

1. Read a good reference book about the Bible. Get a little background yourself. Here are a few good suggestions:

Ryrie's Concise Guide to the Bible by Charles C. Ryrie (Here's Life Publishers)

Evidence That Demands a Verdict by Josh McDowell (Here's Life Publishers)

Can I Trust the Bible? by Howard F. Vos (Moody Press)

How to Understand the Bible by Ralph Herring and Frank Stagg (Broadman)

The Bible Speaks to Today's World by C. Welton Gaddy (Broadman)

You might even be interested in studying right along with your child. There are a number of good adult Bible correspondence courses available from the following publishers:

Navpress (ministry of the Navigators), Box 1659, Colorado Springs, Colorado 80901

Roper Press, 6441-M Gaston, Dallas, Texas 75214

Liberty Home Bible Institute, Box 1111, Lynchburg, Virginia 24505

Campus Crusade for Christ, Arrowhead Springs, San Bernardino, California 92414

Through the Bible Radio, Box 100, Arroyo Annex, Pasadena, California 91109

2. Give a Bible as a gift to your youngster. One wise mom I know marked key verses with a yellow marking pen. When her daughter Jenny received the book, the "landmark" verses stood out plainly, and were the first and most often perused. Jenny was also given a marking pen of her own to continue coloring in her favorite verses over the years ahead.

3. Help your child become familiar with the new Bible. No one would dream of taking a child to a public library and assuming he would learn to use it all alone. Leaving a child unattended in God's library of sixty-six books is not good common sense either. Plan for some uninterrupted time, and leaf through the new Bible together. Show your child how to find his way around God's Word. Point out the Old and New Testaments. Count the books in each. Demonstrate how a written reference leads directly to a specific passage. Look up favorite stories and find old friends — David and Goliath, the wise men in the Christmas story, Daniel in the lions' den.

4. Motivate your child to study God's Word. Include with the Bible an extra surprise — a sealed envelope containing a message similar to this one: "Look in the den closet for a package with your name on it. You may open the package after you have recited the names of the books of the Old Testament perfectly to any adult in the family. Now look in the top dresser drawer for another surprise."

Have a smaller box, just as carefully and intriguingly wrapped there. The card on it should say, "You may open this box after you have recited the names of all the New Testament books." You might also want to include in the box a "Books of the Bible" bookmark, puzzle or ruler as a starter. Or offer a reward for every six names of the books of the Bible memorized.

5. *And finally, don't stop now!* You've only just begun. You've opened the door to sharing your faith and God's great truths with your child. Now follow through. Set time aside and enjoy many more Bible learning activities ahead.

Suggested Get-Acquainted Activities

Select-A-Verse

Stuff an envelope or empty recipe box with about fifty file cards. Have a favorite Scripture reading typed on each. Let your child have the fun of drawing one each night before bed and reading it aloud.

How We Got Our Bibles

Show pictures of the Dead Sea or other scrolls. Talk about how God spoke to many men, and how they wrote what God said on rolled-up pieces of parchment. Explain the wonder of so many writers living so far apart in time and space, yet all writing the same message from God. And finally, talk about how

God has miraculously preserved His Word through the centuries. A good story to look up and read is found in Jeremiah 36. It tells of a wicked king who tried to destroy God's Word but couldn't.

What Do I Read When I'm . . .?

Help your child copy this list onto a blank page of his or her new Bible.

What do I read when I'm sad?	Hebrews 2:18 Habakkuk 3:17-19 Psalm 43:5
What do I read when I'm happy?	Psalm 33:20,21 Psalm 106:3 Psalm 104:33-35
What do I read when I'm lonesome?	Psalm 54:4 John 14:15-18 Romans 8:38,39
What do I read when I'm bored?	Psalm 17:15
What do I read when I'm discouraged?	Romans 8:28 I Corinthians 2:9 Isaiah 43:2

Prophecy and Fulfillment

Use this activity to point out Jesus in the Old Testament as well as in the New. Talk about the Old Testament writers who predicted events in Jesus' life, then look up the corresponding passages in the New Testament where the predicted events came true.

Prophecy		Fulfillment
Born in Bethlehem	Micah 5:2	Matthew 2:1
Miracles	Isaiah 35:5,6	Mark 7:33-35 Matthew 9:32,33,35

Betrayal	Psalm 41:9	John 13:21
Beaten and spit on	Isaiah 50:6	Matthew 26:67
Resurrection	Psalm 16:10	Acts 2:31

Scribble Wall

Post a large sheet of colored plastic or oilcloth on a wall of your child's room. Have an understanding that everything that goes on it must relate somehow to the Bible. Provide water-soluble, non-toxic markers and a damp wiping cloth. Keep the scribble sheet active by suggesting fun after-school, Bible-related activities. Stimulate two-way communication. Here are a few examples:

Did you know Stephen was stoned to death? See Acts 6:8-15 and Acts 7:54-60.

Who is the world's oldest man? Write his name here:_____ How long did he live? _____ Where did he live? _____ (See Genesis 5.)

The sun stopped once. Read about it in Joshua 10. Write below in ten words or less what happened.

Which Bible story shall we read before bed tonight? Write the reference on paper and tape it to your bedroom door before 8 p.m.

I love you. See note inside bread box for a way to earn an extra cream puff. (Note says, ''Any time before Saturday night, you can take a cream puff from the freezer when you can say the books of the Bible perfectly.

EXTRA!!! Christ will return to earth one day. Read all about it in Matthew 24, 1 Thessalonians 5:1-10, and Revelation 19:11-16.

Surprise Treats

Occasionally put a note on the cookie jar (or any other appropriate place) that says, "Two free cookies at any time today for anyone who has read the Bible for at least ten minutes."

Check-Off Poster

Make ·a reading schedule of verses or chapters with rewards marked off at different intervals. Post the schedule in your child's room, and let him check off each passage as he reads it. A "grand finale" treat might be lunch at McDonalds.

Bible Activity Box

An activity box is a tool to get kids learning by themselves. It is one of the best ways available to inject some Bible into youngsters while they are having fun. A Bible Activity Box is really a grab bag of assignments for children to work on alone.

To make an activity box, buy twenty large manila envelopes. Number each envelope, and place a secret assignment along with a reward for completion inside each. Stand envelopes on end in a cardboard box. Let your child draw one of the envelopes, complete the assignment, and earn the reward on his own.

The activity box does not require a hovering parent. Somehow, the idea of choosing to do secret assignments apart from parental suggestion or coercion is intriguing to kids.

And the box promotes positive attitudes about working with Scripture because each association with the Bible is fun and yields plenty of quick rewards. Below are some possibilities for envelope contents. Others can be easily contrived to fit your child's personality and preferences.

1. Enclose a piece of paper that says: "Set the timer for 15 minutes. See if you can memorize Psalm 23:1-3 in that time. Ask Mom for super-duper treat."

2. Write one letter of the alphabet on each page of a small notebook. Ask the child to write the books of the Bible that begin with each letter on the appropriate page. You might also ask for the page number the book begins on in his Bible.

3. Place a small magnifying glass in the envelope with the instructions: "Read the book of Titus, using this magnifying glass."

4. Put several colored sheets of paper in the envelope with these instructions: "Copy good, helpful Bible verses on six of your favorite colored sheets. Do you like popcorn while you work? See Mom."

5. Place these instructions in an envelope: "Read the story of creation (Genesis, chapters 1 and 2) or read about Noah (Genesis 6,7,8 and 9) and then draw a picture showing as many details as you can. Two hugs for each authentic detail. Can you keep me hugging all evening?"

6. Put a small pen-size flashlight in one envelope with these instructions: "After dark, get in bed and read one of the exciting stories listed below."

Acts 27	Paul's shipwreck
Acts 12:1-20	Peter's escape from prison
I Samuel 19 and 20	Jonathan saving David
Mark 6:1-56	Jesus feeding 5000

7. Write on a sheet of paper: "Read any chapter of the Bible and tell what it is about. Ask Mom for the 'secret something' on the top shelf of her closet when you finish. No peeking allowed!"

8. Give these directions: "Make a Bible verse bookmark for Grandma. Enclose it in the pretty card in the dining room bureau, third drawer down, left side."

9. Enclose a Bible picture and these instructions: "Cut up the enclosed picture and make a puzzle. Put the puzzle back together and memorize the verse on the back. Look in Dad's old bathrobe pocket for red, white and blue scissors, jumbo pencil and brand new tablet to work with."

10. Instructions for this envelope could read: "Make a Bible verse picture to hang on the cupboard door. Extra bonus if it contains at least 25 words and if you memorize the verse. Must be neat!"

11. Make up a book of coupons and staple them together. The coupons can say things like:

"This coupon good for six and 7/8 cents when you can say John 3:16. Want more? Try memorizing Psalm 40:17 and Hebrews 4:13."

"This coupon good for your choice of fruit, or a secret story about once when Dad got spanked, when you have read John 1:1-29. Caution: This coupon is only good during months that begin with the letters, J,A,F or D!"

"This coupon good for double allowance when you have read Matthew, Mark, Luke or John all the way through."

"This coupon good for one free room-cleaning after you read the whole book of John in seven days or less. (Let Mom know the day you begin reading.)"

Supportive Activities

By adolescence, a youngster ought to have established a daily pattern of private Bible reading and prayer, and be as familiar with the Book of books as he is with the dictionary. It is, after all, his handbook for successful Christian living. Many varied activities will insure continued interest in the Word of God. Listed below are several Bible-related activities to help you meet this constant need.

Bible Correspondence Courses

Many publishers have excellent graded children's correspondence studies. Most ask only for a donation to their ministries. Shortly after giving my daughter her new Bible, I wrote to the Billy Graham Follow-Up Department, and asked that Gale be enrolled in their children's home Bible study course, *Trusting Jesus.* Sure enough, a few days later, a beautiful little study booklet came in the mail. Gale eagerly used her new Bible to fill in the blanks, and sent the first lesson back, knowing she would get more mail in return. Her lesson was checked and sent back to her even before she got Lesson #2 sent along. For several weeks, Gale enthusiastically pursued her self-help journey into Scripture. The best part was that it took no daily pushing from me. The pre-planning was enough. She wanted to do it by herself in spare moments and would most often pick it up when bored. Her motivation was the new Bible, a smidgen of knowledge about it, and a brightly-colored Billy Graham study guide. Here are just a few of the publishers who offer this type of service:

Billy Graham, Follow-Up Department, Box 779, Minneapolis, Minnesota 55440

Mailbox Bible Club, 237 Fairfield Avenue, Upper Darby, Pennsylvania 19082

Child Evangelism Fellowship Inc., Box 348, Warrenton, Missouri 63383

Emmaus Correspondence School, 156 North Oak Park Avenue, Oak Park, Illinois 60301

Campus Crusade for Christ, Arrowhead Springs, San Bernardino, California 92414

Bible Clubs

You might want to consider sponsoring a weekly after school or Saturday Bible club. Both Child Evangelism Fellowship and Bible Club have trained teachers in many areas who will come by invitation to a home to teach neighborhood children about Christ. (Look in the phone book for their number in your area.) They usually ask nothing but that you provide a garage, basement, or den, and perhaps a few cookies and Kool Aid for the weekly meetings. Their materials include a wide range of flannelgraph stories, books, songs and Bible memory programs. And their teachers know exactly how to have fun with kids, while recognizing their serious purpose of Bible study. Usually kids will flock to the sessions.

Sponsoring a Bible Club in your home would not only be an effective outreach ministry, but it would also provide a routine, supplemental ministry for your own child.

Cupboard Door Christianity

Keep a constant round of new things posted on the cupboard or refrigerator door. Quotes from the Bible or well-known Christian leaders, human interest items, and cartoons all work well. As long as you keep changing them, your family will keep noticing.

Children's Publications

Freida was the mother of seven- and eight-year-olds. Both children were having trouble learning to read. The teacher had assigned them to read "just anything" they could for nightly practice. So Freida ordered a regular subscription of graded Sunday school papers sent to the house. They included crosswords, comics, cartoons, jokes, Bible-related stories, and fiction just right for each child's reading level. And the subscription did double duty. The kids absorbed the Bible knowledge willingly, and practiced reading at the same time.

Anyone can subscribe to Sunday school papers. They provide cheap, profitable reading, are always interesting, and are graded from kindergarten through high school. The papers are usually shipped once a quarter and average less than five dollars per year. And the kids love getting their own mail!

Search is a magazine published by Bible Club. (See address above.) Besides missionary stories, puzzles, comics, and Bible quizzes, *Search* offers contests with awards for kids who finish the monthly studies.

Audio/Visual Aids

There is a great ministry in cassettes. Christian bookstores carry a wide variety of children's Bible story tapes (and records). On long trips, these are great for taming kids — and adults! They also make good rainy-day, nap or bedtime companions.

Stories That Live, P.O. Box 3591, Tulsa, OK 74135, offers six books and tapes to teach boys and girls the truth about creation, the miracles of Jesus and the love of God.

Many church libraries have projectors and Bible story filmstrips available for check-out. Our Mary Jo often had neighborhood kids sitting cross-legged on the living room floor watching pictures flashed on a blank wall. She even named her dolls Zachariah and Malachi after one such showing!

Viewmaster makes both an inexpensive viewer and a variety of Bible story reels. Projectors and ''talking'' viewers are also available. Projectors and ''talking'' viewers are also available as well as more expensive record players and film viewers. Check your local department and Christian book stores for more information.

Flannelgraph is an effective reinforcer of

Bible knowledge. Have your child retell favorite stories using flannelgraph characters. Children enjoy playing "teacher," gathering their smaller playmates around for a story. If a flannelboard is not available, suggest that they stick the figures on the back of a couch or chair.

Bible Study Helps

Spark an early interest in Bible study. Acquaint your child at a young age with good Bible reference books. Photographs of Bible places, maps, and other helps can heighten interest in Bible study. It is up to the parent to provide the tools as the child becomes old enough and wise enough to use them. Intersperse new material at open points, and pray for God's guidance and help in getting and keeping your child's interest focused upon the Word of God.

A concordance could be a wise gift for your child. Junior-aged kids love the grown-up feeling of being able to use a fat, difficult-looking book to find special information all by themselves. Be sure to purchase a concordance that matches the Bible version your child owns. Try playing "Scotland Yard" with your youngster. Give clues to a certain passage (perhaps two key words). Challenge your young detective to locate the Scripture you are thinking of, using the clues and his new concordance.

Emergency Situations

Scripture (and prayer) can be a wonderful consolation for children as well as for adults. An emergency situation provides a good learning time. One of our girls began to worry about what would happen to her if her father and I both died. When her best friend's father died, the worry sessions increased. So April's daddy held her close in the rocker and said, "Our health is real good. You know how I can beat you in running and skating. We can take good care of you for a very long time. But best of all, God goes on forever."

April sat quietly for a while, then said, "But I am afraid to die, too." Again her father answered, "God promised eternal life to all who believe in His Son. In this house we are all believers. You can trust God. When He says something, that settles it." Then he read to her from Romans 8:11 and John 3:16.

After the reading, April rocked quietly on his lap for a while. Then she said simply, "I think I will go ride my bike now." Her worries had subsided. She had been well taught in the arms of a loving father about where to go for comfort in a time of need. When emergencies arise in your family, try to make your reactions include demonstrations of faith in God and in His Word. Remember, actions speak louder than words. Show your children an active faith in emergency situations.

Chapter 2

How to Teach Your Child to Pray

"And it came about that while He was praying in a certain place, after He had finished, one of His disciples said to Him, 'Lord, teach us to pray. . .'"

—Luke 11:1

"When I saw my wife on LSD, senseless, first in a stupor, then mumbling, then shouting, then begging for help from imagined demons chasing her, then screaming, I was chilled with fear. What would I do? We were an hour back from the main trail up in the northern Georgia mountains. There was no one around for miles. So I told her we would pray. Neither of us knew how. She finally said she remembered a little prayer her mother had taught her. It was all we knew. . . 'Lord I am a sinner. Forgive me.'

33

Somehow, it quieted us both to be in contact with God, even briefly. My wife relaxed there on the ground. I put my arms tight around her, and we went into a deep sleep, in midday with a grassy mud mound for a pillow. It was enough. God heard. He delivered us both from drugs right then." This is the testimony of a 25-year-old man concerning the usefulness of childhood prayer.

Childhood prayers are not trivia. Good prayer habits taught to youngsters remain throughout adulthood. However, many adults responsible for training children feel confident without God, and rarely talk to Him in prayer. When things are going well, we often do not seem to need God, and it is easy to forget to communicate with Him throughout the day. Many of us wait until a problem arises, or until tragedy occurs, before we disrupt our routines for a moment of prayer. And then, when we finally do take time to pray, too often we hurriedly stumble before the throne of grace, mumbling a "forgive me for my sins" preface, hoping we have thereby won the favor and blessing of God. Shame on us if we pass along to our children such a haphazard, unscriptural approach to prayer!

A routine prayer life is not acquired automatically with salvation. It is something that develops through discipline, through an understanding of the privilege and power of prayer, and by exercising that privilege frequently. Once a parent establishes a regular prayer life, it will be easy to pass it along to his children. But even the disciples who knew the Son of God personally, felt a lack. One asked, "Lord, teach us to pray" (Luke 11:1). And so we also should ask that He not only teach *us* to pray, but that He help us to teach our children to pray.

Here are some general principles to pass along to children of all ages. Some of these are discussed in greater detail later in the chapter.

1. Prayer is talking to God (Luke 11:2; Philippians 1:3,4: Ephesians 3:14).
2. God hears our prayers (Psalm 116:1,2; 145:18,19; Jeremiah 29:12,13; I Peter 3:12; I John 5:14,15).
3. God answers our prayers (Isaiah 65:24; Ephesians 1:19,20).
4. We can pray any time (Psalm 55:1,16,17).
5. We can pray anywhere (Psalm 139:1-12; Jonah 2:1).
6. We can pray in any way — silently, out loud, short or long, in any position, in any language (Joshua 5:14; I Samuel 1:13; I Kings 8:22; 2 Chronicles 6:13; Acts 20:36).
7. We can pray about anything (Hebrews 4:16).
8. Prayer is not an option — it is a privilege, a responsibility and a command (Luke 18:1; 21:36; Ephesians 6:18; I Thessalonians 5:17).

Praying With Your Children

Praying together over important matters can start early. Take, for instance, the example of a couple in New York State whose six-year-old was having problems in school. As the mother and I sat together over a late morning cup of coffee at the kitchen table, Robbie came into the room with his coat on. He was ready to leave for afternoon kindergarten. It was wonderful to watch as Robbie's mom put her arm around the boy and prayed with him about the day ahead. "Lord, you know Robbie has trouble sitting quietly," she said. "Calm him down today. Remind him often that he needs to stay in his seat. And keep his chatter down too. Miss Stone needs his help." Then she planted a king-size kiss on the child's cheek and sent him off to school with an attitude of "bring on the day!" The mother told me that they had been praying together daily for a month. And she showed me a note from the teacher telling of Robbie's improvement. What a lucky child!

Praying Any Time

The very best kind of prayer is spontaneous. A child ought to be able to listen to a grown-up Christian whose prayer is simply a conversation with God. Children should realize that prayer is just talking to God, straight from the heart.

Have you ever stopped baking cookies or put down a hammer to pray with your child? That is how to teach a child to pray — when the opportunity presents itself. "Lord, we love you and know you watch us all the time and are interested in everything we do. Now help

Daddy this afternoon as he goes to see the boss in the meeting. Put words in his mouth that will be just right. You can do that just fine, and we trust You for it. You know his job depends on it.''

Or how about in the middle of the night when your child awakens, afraid? It may not be easy giving a lesson on prayer in the wee hours of the morning, but it will be an effective and invaluable lesson. You will have shown confidence in the Lord and His ability to help in a time of need. And how about after a disruptive argument? Or before school or before a trip to the doctor's office? How about when a beloved pet is lost or dying? The important thing is to show a child that God can always be reached at a moment's notice.

Praying Anywhere

Many people insist that absolute quiet is necessary for prayer. Quietness does promote reverence and clear minds, and we need times of quiet prayer (Psalm 46:10; Isaiah 30:15). But quietness is not a prerequisite for prayer — and it's a good thing — because silence is a premium commodity in our busy world.

Teach children that God can be reached from anywhere — a sun deck or a storm cellar; while swimming under water or flying above the clouds; in the velvet padded pew of a beautiful church or in a rickety folding chair in a half-constructed basement. God hears and answers prayers from anywhere in the whole wide world.

Bible Examples of Praying from Various Places

II Samuel 7:1,2,18-29	King David from inside a tent
I Kings 8:22	King Solomon from inside temple
I Kings 18:19,36,37	Elijah on a mountain
I Kings 19:4	Elijah under a tree
II Kings 6:8-17	Elisha in the dark
Daniel 4:33-35	Nebuchadnezzer from a field
Jonah 2:1-9	Jonah from a fish's belly
Acts 16:13	Women by a river
Acts 16:23-25	Paul in prison

Praying in Any Way

We can pray in any way — silently, out loud, short or long, on our knees, on our heads or standing up. There are many different methods and positions illustrated in the Bible.

We can pray all by ourselves, or take turns with another person. Large numbers of people can pray together by listening closely and silently, agreeing with what is being said. Even small children can learn early that they can help in group praying. To do this, they need to be told to pay attention and to think the same prayer thoughts as the adults. I heard a small child on her mother's lap in church utter, "Yes, Lord Jesus" during a prayer for comfort for a bereaved family the child knew well. She had learned to consider herself an important part of the group. She felt responsible not to entertain wandering thoughts.

Bible Examples of Praying in Different Ways

Joshua 5:14	Joshua on his face before God
I Samuel 1:13	Hannah praying silently
2 Chronicles 6:13	King Solomon kneeling
Matthew 26:39	Jesus lying on the ground
Luke 18:11-13	Pharisee using lots of words; publican using very few
Luke 23:46	Jesus with a loud voice
Daniel 2:17,18 Acts 12:5-17	Groups praying

Praying About Anything

We should also teach children that anyone can pray to God about anything. Prayer is saying to God whatever is on your mind. Dr. James T. Dyet illustrates this principle by using Hebrews 4:16 and this story: A primary Sunday school teacher asked her class for prayer requests. One little girl asked for prayer because she was apprehensive about spending the summer with her real mother. The teacher shied away from the broken home saying, ''We don't pray about things like that.'' Another little boy was going to visit his grandparents, and Grandpa's horse had bitten him. So he wanted prayer that the horse would not bite him again. Once more the teacher replied, ''We only pray about big things, not little things like that.'' And yet, Dr. Dyet instructs, the writer of Hebrews said to ''come boldly before the throne of grace'' (KJV), implying in the original text that we are to ''speak our minds,'' ''to hold nothing back.'' Thank God for children who do not feel silly asking their heavenly Father for help — even if it just concerns a cranky old horse on Grandpa's farm!

Teaching the Young Child

A mother who holds a young child on her lap and prays aloud teaches the child how to pray. He sees her reverence, her closed eyes, her beseeching and sincere attitude. He notes that she speaks in ordinary language to her friend, God. A father who prays aloud in a strong, deep voice before meals shows his family his faith in God. It may be that a four- or five-year-old will not understand all the words in family prayers, but he will learn much about the procedure of prayer.

But even a young child needs the opportunity and encouragement to pray — before any ideas of feeling silly or embarrassed have a chance to take root. To begin, the parent may have to put words in the mouth of a very young child. However, it is important to encourage the youngster to pray for himself as soon as he is able. And when that happens, let his words flow without comment even though the prayers may be bungling efforts and may sound funny to adult ears. One four-year-old thanked the Lord for the "roast beast" on the supper table!

Keep in mind that when Jesus said, "Let the children alone, and do not hinder them from coming to Me" (Matthew 19:14), He no doubt was including their coming to Him in childhood prayer.

Teaching Older Children

Start by reading Dr. Bill Bright's booklet, *How to Pray* (Campus Crusade for Christ). Dr. Bright suggests the A-C-T-S formula:

> Adoration
>
> Confession
>
> Thanksgiving
>
> Supplication

Discuss and practice these basic prayer principles using the guidelines in the rest of this chapter. You might want to hang the A-C-T-S letters up in your child's room to remind him of this prayer process. Cut them from construction paper. Mount and frame them; or make a mobile. Refer to the A-C-T-S formula often as you pray with your child.

Adoration

Webster's New Collegiate Dictionary defines adoration as the ''act of paying honor to a divine being'' or ''homage paid to one held in high esteem.'' Obviously, in order to adore God, one must know He is someone worthy of adoration and honor. So the first step in teaching adoration is to give children a reason to worship. They must begin to realize who God is, what He has already done for them, and what He has promised to do for those who love and serve Him.

Carlyle said, "Wonder is the basis of all worship." No one lives in a world of wonderment more than children. What an opportune time to introduce them to the wonders of their Savior and Lord! Begin to teach the attributes of God — not by hammering them into the child's memory one by one, but by commenting on God's great love, or by pointing out His handiwork in creation or by exhibiting your confidence in His great power. Talk about the God who sees everyone everywhere all the time. Tell of the God who knows how many hairs are on each head; who designs every snowflake we sled through in winter; who calls each twinkling star at night by name.

Read Psalms 138, 139, 145-150, Job 38 and 39, and Ephesians 3:18 and 19. And then work some phrases — not sermons or treatises — of adoration into your prayers. Remember that children learn by example — good examples — examples that are clear and relevant to them:

> "Lord, I'm glad you're God and that You can watch over me no matter where I am or what I'm doing."

> "Father, I know that no one but You could make our roses smell so sweet."

Confession

Confession is the means to an effective prayer life. Many Scriptures indicate that God does not promise even to hear the prayers of the iniquitous, let alone answer them (Psalm 66:17-20; John 9:31). But the prayers of a forgiven, righteous man unleash the unlimited power of God (Psalm 84:11; James 5:16; I John 3:21,22; 5:14,15).

If confession is the key, we need to understand exactly what confession is and practice it regularly. And more than that, we must instruct our children so they too can experience productive, powerful prayer lives. To "confess" is to "say the same thing" about sin that God says, or to take the same attitude toward sin that God takes. God hates sin and excludes it from His presence.

What is sin? Probably the best explanation for children is found in James 4:17. Sin is all the wrong things we do. And we should hate doing wrong and strive to exclude wrongdoing from our daily lives. But when we fail and do wrong, or sin, we should agree with God that what we did was wrong — sin — and ask His forgiveness. Psalm 51 is an excellent example of true confession. It shows David's abhorrent attitude toward his sin, and the contrite spirit necessary for forgiveness.

Teach the principles of confession both by word and example. And teach that confession can be made anywhere and any time . . . in bed, at play, while soaking in the tub, or washing the car or on your knees. A child should know that a person who confesses sin to God and repents of it, is a powerful person because God listens to the prayers of a forgiven individual.

Most children will be reluctant to confess wrongdoing in your presence just as you would be hesitant to confess your faults in theirs! So have a time of silent, prayerful confession. Then help your child realize the love and forgiveness we experience as a result of confession. After the time of silent prayer, you might pray aloud: "God, I am clean before you. I have confessed my sin as far as I know it. You said You would forgive, and I believe it. I'll try not to do those wrong things anymore. . . ."

Even a child who confesses sin regularly can move the hands of God through prayer. God listens to the person made clean through the blood of Christ.

Thanksgiving

Saying "thank you" is one of the first social graces we impose upon our children. But true thankfulness is more than just saying "thank you." True thankfulness and the expression of that gratitude spring from a realization that someone has done something for you. Thankfulness is an attitude (Psalm 9:1); saying "thank you" is one way to acknowledge a kindness or favor.

Psalm 50:14 says, "Offer to God a sacrifice of thanksgiving. . . ." Hebrews 13:15 says, "Through Him then, let us continually offer up a sacrifice of praise to God, that is, the fruit of lips that give thanks to His name."

Sacrifices are offerings, willingly given to God in recognition of His superiority. Sacrifices are not free, but require the offerer to give up something, or to give of himself. Why, then, would giving thanks be a "sacrifice?"

Most everyone has the experience sooner or later of attempting to evoke a "thank you" from a child. Perhaps a lady at a cash register has offered your child a sucker. Johnny grabbed the sucker, popped it in his mouth and headed for the door. You grabbed Johnny, stopping him in his tracks, and said, "What do you tell this nice lady?" Nothing. "Can you tell the lady, 'Thank you'?" you chide. Obviously not. After several attempts, *you* told her thank you and marched your child out the door to the tune of Lecture #247: "That lady was nice enough to give you a sucker. The least you could have done was tell her 'Thank you'!"

But for little Johnny to thank the lady would have required several things on his part — sacrifices, so to speak. First of all, he would have had to realize that she had done something nice for him. And probably he did. But in order for him to express his gratitude, he would have had to interrupt his sucker-sucking session, pull the candy out of his mouth and exercise his vocal cords.

It might have been that Johnny didn't see any need to thank the lady. Perhaps he felt she *owed* him the sucker. Or maybe, since he didn't get the particular flavor he wanted, Johnny didn't see any need to be thankful. Or maybe Johnny didn't say, "Thank you," because it would have embarrassed him. And besides, why should he say, "Thank you," for such a little thing?

Although these are all invalid excuses and reflect an attitude of ingratitude, many children and adults are just as reluctant to offer thanks to God. We don't appreciate the many good things He gives us because we expect them; we feel God *owes* them to us. Or perhaps we are not quite as thankful as we should be because God failed to give us the particular kind of favor we wanted; or because the kindness He bestowed upon us was just a little one. And it is difficult to interrupt our busy lives just to say "thank you." And maybe we fail to give thanks as we should because it involves a sacrifice of pride to bow before His throne and admit that He has done more for us than we could ever do for ourselves.

Teaching and nurturing true thankfulness then, is not an easy task. Thankfulness should be willingly offered to God as we recognize His supreme care for us. Try to practice giving thanks for everything (Colossians 4:17) all the time (Ephesians 5:20), and encourage the same in the lives of your children. Be the leader in thanksgiving as Mattaniah was (Nehemiah 11:17). Set an example at mealtime as Jesus and Paul did (Mark 8:6; Acts 27:35).

And so as David did. Appoint others — your children included — to express thankfulness to the Lord (I Chronicles 16:7).

Supplication

Supplication is nearly automatic. Wanting things and asking for them is natural. The hungry cry of a newborn or the grasping hand of a toddler are not learned habits — they are inborn traits. And "Gimme, gimme, gimme," is the battlecry of the whole human race.

But supplication is more than just asking. It is the act of making a sincere, *humble* request before God. It is based on our need and His ability to supply that need. And supplication necessarily follows confession (Psalm 66:17-20).

Jesus and the apostle John related supplication to our familial relationship with our heavenly Father. A child has needs. A father has both the responsibility and desire to meet the needs of his child as long as the requests do not interfere with the overall welfare of that child.

John wrote that we become children of God through faith. Because of that relationship, we know our Father hears our requests and meets our needs according to His will (I John 5:14,15). Jesus said we know earthly fathers give good things to their children, and because we know that, we should automatically expect our heavenly Father to give us much better things in response to our requests (Matthew 7:7-11). What an easy comparison for even a small child to understand! And how automatic for them to turn to another Father to ask for the things they need and want.

Guard against making supplication the most important or lengthiest part of prayer. Precede it with honest confession before God. And balance it with the proper amounts of adoration and thanksgiving. Use these verses to help teach the "asking for things" part of prayer: Ephesians 3:18-20; 6:18; Philippians 4:6; and James 4:2,3.

Resource Materials

For parents who want to learn more about the power of prayer and prayer procedure, I suggest writing to Change The World Ministry, P.O. Box 5838, Mission Hills, CA 91345 or Campus Crusade for Christ, Arrowhead Springs, San Bernardino, CA 92414. Both organizations present "How to Pray" seminars and will send current lists of urgent prayer matters from around the world as well as booklets on the subject. The seminars teach about creative ways to pray, obstacles to prayer, and the power of prayer.

Prayer Adventures for Boys and Girls, P.O. Box 8535, Fountain Valley, CA 92708 will help train boys and girls in effective prayer. Children are challenged to become watchers in daily prayer.

The following books might also prove valuable in teaching your child to pray:

How I Know God Answers Prayer by Rosalind Goforth (Moody Press).

I Can Pray To God by Sandra Brooks (Standard). A child's first book on prayer.

Prayer: Conversing with God by Rosalind Rinker (Zondervan).

Prayers for Families by Barbara Own Webb (Judson Press).

Teaching Your Child to Pray by Colleen Townsend Evans (Doubleday). A book you and your young child can read together.

What Happens when Women Pray by Evelyn Christianson (Victor Books).

With Christ in the School of Prayer by Andrew Murray (Moody Press).

Chapter 3

Creative Family Worship

". . . but as for me and my house, we will serve the Lord."

—Joshua, in Joshua 24:25

There is unity in a family on its knees before God. Every member senses there is a higher authority to be heeded. Humanistic self-dependence is left far behind when the overwhelming presence of God and His peace are felt. Touching elbows with other lives yielded to God helps reinforce allegiance to Him and to each other.

But unfortunately, many moms and dads resist routine family worship. To them, the idea suggests interminable Bible reading and lengthy prayer. They may have been unwilling audiences when they were children, and they remember unintelligible, adult-oriented "family" altars.

Others deem family worship old-timey, boring, or ineffective. Some may have actually tried family worship for a while only to find the time more of an endurance test than an anticipated event.

Whatever the case, most parents agree that home is the prime learning place and worship is the spiritual force that binds a family together. And all believe that today's families need warm and close dimensions to face successfully a world of crumbling relationships.

A home devotional time offers parents a natural place to share scriptural truths and great Bible doctrines. Children can be taught to respond to God in faith with holiness and obedience. And with just a little planning, family worship can be intriguing enough to keep the whole family interested, learning, and worshiping. Creativity and ingenuity are the keys to success. Here are some challenging ideas to help you.

The Beginner or the Expert

Maybe you're just thinking about beginning family worship in your home. Or maybe you've tried and failed. Or maybe you're an old hand at family devotions. Whatever your situation or level of expertise, attitude and expectations are all-important.

Be realistic. Unload the phony family altar image of super-spiritual parents leading angelic cherubs in formal mini-church services at home. Kids are bound to whine when called in from play. Little hands will get into trouble when others' eyes are closed in prayer. Attention spans are sometimes short and active minds tend to wander. Expect times of failure. But when they come, don't use them as an excuse for quitting. Accept them as typical and begin to search for something new, something that will recapture interest. This chapter is filled with many ideas, tried and proven in ordinary family homes like yours.

Remember to pray specifically that the Holy Spirit will work through your efforts so the family will grow into Christian maturity. Ask often that He speak to the needs of each individual and that each draws from the daily worship experience what is lacking in his life for that day. Claim often the promise that He "is able to do exceeding abundantly beyond all that we ask or think, according to the power that works within us" (Ephesians 3:20).

If your family has not had a time of worship together before, introduce it gradually. Help your children enjoy devotions. It is, after all, a time in the day when they will have your full attention. Although it's not a play time, fresh, new, Bible-related materials and books can be included to make worship time varied and pleasant for all family members, regardless of age. Keep the worship time short. Stop when interest is high. Refuse to let family worship be grim or boring. (One family keeps a game of chess going from day to day as the group gathers!)

Family worship can be underplanned or overplanned, be too spontaneous or too contrived. It can be fun, inspirational, interesting, informative or just plain dull, depending on the resourcefulness of the person in charge. Try to discover and use new and different ideas, materials — even times and places. And find out how other families make their worship time workable.

The Time

The gathering to worship will never happen without a plan. Choose a time when the family is unhurried and relaxed. Breakfast or dinner times have been traditional favorites but with today's frantic schedules, other times may be more convenient. Occasionally duplicate sessions may be necessary to accommodate everyone.

Family worship must be steady — day after day, week after week, month after month. Let the family know it is a routine occurrence — one that is just as natural as eating, scheduled just as regularly and planned just as well. Expect days when the worship time will have to be cut short. But don't despair. Daily constancy will compensate.

Your family worship time will be riddled with as many — or as few — interruptions as you choose to allow. Most interferences can be handled quickly, postponed for a few minutes, or avoided altogether. Make up your mind that nothing short of a life-threatening emergency will interrupt family worship. Unplug the phone. Put the dog outside. Feed and change the baby. Send little ones to the bathroom before you begin. And let neighborhood playmates know that Johnny cannot play at such-and-such a time each day. Anticipate problems and work around them. Make the small block of time scheduled for family worship the most important time of the day.

The Place

Hold family devotions in various places for a pleasant change of scenery. . . on the back patio when the azaleas are in bloom, at the kitchen table, in the den or living room, in front of a glowing fireplace, in a circle on the rug, in a newly wallpapered room, on a porch swing watching a sunset, around one family member's sickbed or in a boat on vacation. Let family members try to come up with unusual places to meet around the Word of God.

The Program

The program and the methods of presenting the program should be as varied as the snowflakes in a winter storm. While having the same general content and goals, each gathering should be meaningful and interesting. The basic ingredients should be the same — worship, Bible-reading, Scripture memorization and prayer — but the garnishing should be spectacular! Kind of like your favorite oatmeal cookie recipe: the basic ingredients make it good, but the occasional additions of nuts or raisins or chocolate chips make it terrific! Read through the helps which follow and make the basic ingredients for your family worship good. Then throw in "something extra" from the section by that title and begin to reap the delicious blessings successful family worship yields.

Basic Ingredient #1: Worship

Worship is praising, loving, responding in the heart to God; being in awe of who He is; being in a spirit of submission to His will. Worship focuses on God Himself. Thoughts are turned directly to Him in adoration, seeing God in all His wonder and worshiping Him because of it.

Worship is not automatic with children. The attitude of worship must be taught by example and cultivated through experience. Doling out information about God does not necessarily lead a child to worship. Nor does teaching a youngster to recite a list of the attributes of God insure an attitude of worship. If there is no response in the heart, no wonder at who God is, the child is a long way from worshiping and loving the Lord with all his heart, soul and mind (Matthew 22:37).

Since worship is a personal response to God, family devotions should allow for and attempt to elicit this response from each participant. Teach, yes, but then ask for even the youngest child's reaction to his Maker. For example, tell the story of Stephen's martyrdom. Explain God's faithfulness to Stephen even through the terrible stoning. Tell how God gave Stephen a special glimpse of heaven before he died. Discuss God's faithfulness to your family. Ask each child to tell one special thing God has done for him or his family. Then pray together, thanking God for His faithfulness, and asking for the strength and courage to be as brave and faithful as Stephen was.

Each day let the children tell how the Bible lesson applies to their lives and how it makes them feel about God. Stories and other tools can be bland, sterile instruments of teaching, or they can stir up feelings that will result in worship and adoration of God.

Basic Ingredient #2: Bible Reading

Dr. Oswald J. Smith, former pastor of the People's Church in Toronto, Canada, says God's Word should be read daily just as manna was gathered daily. We would not dream of taking only one meal a day, much less per week, to nourish our bodies. So, he reminds us, our spiritual selves need regular feedings, too.

Some families may prefer to start at Genesis 1:1 and read through the Bible. Others may prefer to read through selected books. Acts, accompanied by maps, can be fascinating. The story of Ruth can be followed easily, as can the Gospel of John.

You might want to vary the reading. Sometimes read several chapters in sequence. Other times, choose verses on a single subject scattered throughout the Bible. (Use a concordance for help.) Or use Scripture associated with upcoming Sunday school lessons. Every so often have "favorites week" when family members share their favorite passages. Or for a while, pick passages from the Bible which quote Jesus directly. Use a red letter edition if you have one. Then ask the family to express in their own words just what Jesus said.

Vary methods too. Let each family member take a turn reading on a given night. Allow silent reading occasionally. Let the parents read a verse, then the children and so on. Alternately use a large-print Bible or any other favorite version. Provide yellow marking pens for individuals to underline parts of the Scripture that are especially inspirational or important.

And remember: no matter what plan or methods you are using, you are feeding young minds. Explain the tough places (like all the "begats"), define big words, clarify the basic ideas, and restate in ordinary language any difficult concepts. Make God's Word clear and usable to each person.

Basic Ingredient #3: Scripture Memorization

God commands in Deuteronomy 6:6 and 7a: "And these words, which I am commanding you today, shall be on your heart; and you shall teach them diligently to your sons." Clearly, God's Word should be passed down from generation to generation in such a way that each generation knows it as well as the former generation. And a vital part of this knowledge is the committing of portions of Scripture to memory.

Psalm 1 and Joshua 1:8 tie the successful life and meditating on Scripture together. Since meditating means *mulling over, ruminating,* or *chewing on,* obviously the one who meditates on the Word must become thoroughly acquainted with it. Memorization achieves this kind of familiarity. So, parents who want their children to become successful by God's standards would do well to help them memorize God's Word. Here are some ideas for building fun and interest into the discipline of memorizing Scripture.

• Set up contests between adults and kids. Offer fun prizes. Draw up a "contract." For instance, "If the kids memorize the verses more quickly than the adults, the adults will take out the trash for a week. But if the adults memorize them first, the kids will do the supper cleanup for a week." Be sure to sign the contract to make it official!

• Help little children learn by repetition. Review while rocking, bathing, or playing with them. Repeat while driving, waiting in line at the grocery store, etc. Here are some short verses one of our girls knew before age six:

"God is love" (I John 4:8).
"For all have sinned" (Romans 3:23).
"Christ Jesus came into the world to save sinners"
    (I Timothy 1:15).
"Christ died for our sins" (I Corinthians 15:3).
"I will give you rest" (Matthew 11:28).
"Be kind to one another" (Ephesians 4:32).
"I and the Father are one" (John 10:30).
"He cares for you" (I Peter 5:7).

• Post current memory work on refrigerator, closet door, or kitchen bulletin board. Or stretch a "clothesline" and clothespin verses for the month to it.

• Have memory charts. Award stickers, stars or seals for each learned verse, prizes for every five stickers.

• Purchase a Scripture songbook and sing Bible verses right into the minds of the family. Or make up your own music for favorite verses.

• Use flannelgraph letters or verse flashcards. Mix up letters and words and take turns straightening them out.

• Write the verse on a chalkboard. Take turns erasing one word at a time. Repeat the whole verse after each erasure.

• Print different verses on 5 x 8 cards. Cut each card into pieces. Put the pieces for each verse in an envelope. Pass out the envelopes and use a timer to see who can put their verse-puzzle together the most quickly. Have each member read his assembled verse.

• Let the leader begin quoting a verse, stopping after every few words to ask another person to add the next four words, or two words, and so on. Have a stick of gum or a lollipop ready for the first person to identify where the verse is located.

• Let the small children use magic markers to print the verse of the week on sheets of construction paper. Add stickers or magazine pictures and use for placemats at dinner.

• Give each youngster an empty photo album with see-through plastic pages. Insert weekly memory cards for an individual record of verses learned and for easy private review.

• For children from ages three or four up to adult who really catch the fun of memorizing, write Bible Memory Association, Box

12000, St. Louis, MO 63112. This organization offers prizes and other incentives for people who commit passages of the Bible to memory. Several other publishers offer convenient, inexpensive Scripture memory packets. Write Navpress, Box 1659, Colorado Springs, CO 80901 and Campus Crusade for Christ, San Bernardino, CA 92414 for information.

• Once in a while assign short Scripture verses to be memorized by the following day. Celebrate completion of the assignment with a yummy treat.

Basic Ingredient #4: Prayer

Prayer is vital to family devotions, so make prayer time meaningful. Keep prayers brief. Make certain they concern what is going on in family life and the world right then. Include requests, praise, and thanks. Pray in ordinary language, avoiding the archaic "Thee" and "Thou." If your family does not feel comfortable kneeling, don't kneel. Praying can be done in any position — out loud or silently — and children should know that.

Pray specifically. Avoid generalities. Rather than praying, "God, help Grandpa," ask God to give Grandpa the special patience he needs to get used to his new bifocals. Specific prayers are fervent prayers. And fervent prayers accomplish much (James 5:16). Such intimacy brings us closer to people, developing compassion and understanding of their problems. Some families enjoy keeping a prayer diary listing dates requests were made, new developments in situations being prayed about, items of praise and answers to specific requests.

And remember, prayer time is not the time to lay out before God the shortcomings of other family members. Prayer time is not the time to sermonize. It is not a time to remind God that "Jack was a naughty boy today, Lord, so we need to pray for him!" Make prayer time a special time when hearts are united in love before the throne of grace.

Something Extra

Use these ideas to add extra sparkle to your family worship time. You'll find each helpful suggestion a delightful change of pace.

• Take turns acting out favorite Bible stories and let other family members guess the identity of the characters involved. Or use puppets. For extra fun, make a home movie of the charades and let the children invite their friends for a premier showing.

• Use "The Muffin Family" section of *Moody Monthly* magazine — fun reading for children, plus creative kinds of Bible quizzes for them to do.

• End devotions with a popcorn party. Or have ingredients ready for do-it-yourself sundaes.

• Watch for terms in the Bible reading that lend themselves to dictionary research. Try to think on your child's level. (One of our daughters thought for years a ''high priest'' was a pastor on a very tall chair. Think how an early introduction to a Bible dictionary would have cleared that up!) And remember to make ''looking it up'' a prestigious role rather than an arduous task. Work similarly with Bible maps, concordances and commentaries from time to time.

• Begin worship time by alerting everyone that after the Bible reading each will be given the chance to stump someone else with a question from the text. Or ask a question or two before the Bible reading and have everyone listen for the answers. Or write questions poster-fashion and have everyone read silently to find the answers.

• Play Bible stories recorded by professional dramatists — Orson Welles or Ethel Barrett, for example.

• Adopt a missionary family. Read prayer letters from them, write answers to them, pray for them, and discuss ways to help meet their special needs.

• If a session gets too long or complicated, excuse younger children for another activity — dot-to-dot Bible books, Bible puzzles, or to color a plastic Bible wall mural.

• Change worship time occasionally to coincide with a favorite religious radio or TV program. Or tape an especially good one for later use. Child Evangelism Fellowship produces a marvelous children's religious fun show called the *Treehouse Club.* CBN, the Christian Broadcasting Network, produces religious programming all day long as does Family Radio. Check local listings for programs in your area.

• Begin by saying, "I am thinking of a verse in Genesis, chapter eight, that talks about a raven." Continue giving hints while the family members search in their Bibles for the correct verse. Have the winner read the verse plus the two verses before and after. For variety, sketch clues on chalkboard or paper.

• Memorize the books of the Bible. Number six envelopes from one to six. Print the names of the first eleven books of the Bible on envelope number one, the next eleven books on envelope number two, and so on. Then cut eleven shapes (stars, triangles, circles and squares are fun) for each envelope. Write the name of each book on a shape and put it in the appropriate envelope. Ask a child to put the shapes in envelope number one in order, using the list on the front. Scramble and repeat. When all eleven books from envelope number one are learned, move on to envelope number two, and so on, until all sixty-six books are learned.

• Use a tape series. Check with your pastor or Christian bookstore for interesting subjects available. Write to Christian Tape Library, 330 N. Range Line Road, Carmel, Indiana, 46032. They lend tapes free, but request donations if possible.

• Use a book of devotions written for children. See the list of suggested volumes at the end of this chapter.

• Once in a while ask each child to come to devotions with something to share: a favorite Scripture, a poem about God, a record, song, or discussion idea. Encourage unusual presentations. One of our children brought a fresh rose and pointed out its marvelous yellow color, delightful odor and the unique structure that God created.

• Purchase a copy of *My Personal Diary* (Scripture Press) for each member of the family. Keep private logs of spiritual adventures. Record what God has been teaching through the experiences He allows in each life. Share special entries from time to time.

• Utilize Sunday school papers. Read a favorite story or joke. (Incidently, Sunday school papers and other Christian publications are terrific bathroom reading material!) One mother bought big notebooks for each of her children to store old Sunday-school papers. She decoupaged the covers using pictures the children thought appropriate. Her kids know she considers the papers important. And the notebooks are often swapped to be read by others in the family.

• Bundle up in slickers, grab an umbrella, and go for a walk in God's rain. Take time to look around, to feel the droplets on your face. Stop and wonder where they came from. Listen to the wind and watch the tree leaves tremble. Make patterns in the mud with your toes and talk about God. Wonder about how He makes the rain. Blow some dandelion fluff and remark about its beauty. Credit God with all of nature around you. And when you get home, share a cup of cocoa and Job 37.

• Watch newspaper ads for upcoming religious events. Many local churches advertise concerts, films and plays they are presenting. Make a night of it. Dress up. Have dinner out before or after. And remember, half the fun is planning ahead and anticipating the special event.

• Talk about current events in light of the Bible. For instance, talk about Israel and the Arab nations. Tell children about Isaac and Ishmael. Show them how that blood feud is still going on between the Jews and the Arabs. Talk about God's future plans for the nations of the world. Build confidence by assuring children that God is in control of the whole world. Even wars and riots can be better understood and more easily accepted with the assurance that it is all part of God's plan. *Youth Faces Today's Issues* by Krutza and DiCicco (Baker) and a subscription to *Bible in the News* (a twenty-four page monthly current events update) will help. Order the latter from Dr. David Webber, Southwest Radio Church, P.O. Box 1144, Oklahoma City, OK 73101.

• Relate or read an interesting true story of the faith. Missionary prayer letters and religious periodicals are good sources.

Play gospel music. Instrumental and vocal selections are available for every musical taste from symphonic to country-western.

• Read the words of a favorite hymn aloud. Discuss what the author was trying to say. Find out something about the author if possible. The great hymns of the faith are our link to other generations who loved the Lord as we do.

• Devote an occasional worship time solely to singing. Take turns leading. Whistle through choruses, clap, sing in harmony, a cappella, or use harmonicas, piano, guitar or other instruments. One family used paper-covered combs and kazoos for a fun variation.

• Let children teach a new song they learned in Sunday school. Have them print the words out for the family ahead of time.

• Record children's choir and play it back. Or use music as a quieter. Have soft music playing as background while the family gathers for worship.

• Show the family a famous religious painting. Ask them to discuss what the artist had in mind. Ask how and why they would make it different if they were the artist. Compare what the picture portrays with what the Bible has to say.

• Have a Bible drill. The leader announces a Bible reference to be located by everyone. Bibles remain closed until he says, ''Draw swords.'' The first to locate the passage stands and reads it aloud.

• When one family member reads an inspirational book, allow time for it to be reviewed. Hopefully others will want to read it too. You might want to devote family worship time for a whole week to silent, individual reading of Christian books. See the suggested reading list at the end of this chapter.

• Make worship a thank you celebration of family events. Celebrate graduations, birthdays, weddings, new babies, relatives visiting, upcoming vacation, when the new church wing is completed, etc. Relate the family affair to appropriate Scripture. Thank God in specific ways for each event. One family celebrated the purchase of a new home by thanking God for the money to buy it, for freedom to choose it and by asking God's guidance in using it to His glory. They sang "Bless This House" and read Joshua 24:14 and 15.

• Buy or make puppets. Have one of the children tell a Bible story using the puppet. An animal puppet could tell an animal story — Noah's ark, Balaam's donkey, or Daniel in the lions' den.

• Families with teens will enjoy Serendipity materials. They are available at most Christian bookstores. Placemats are designed to help each member share some of the current significant events in his life. Try also *Hassle,* a handbook for sixteen family relationship sessions, and *Rap,* a mini-course in personal ethics.

• Invite a missionary family that is home on furlough to tell about their work. Ask a person with an especially intriguing personal testimony to come and share it with the family. Or ask your pastor or youth director to bring devotions one night.

• Plan a picnic. Delay family worship until you are all gathered on a blanket or around a picnic table.

• Subscribe to *Family Life Today,* a magazine designed to help build the Christian family. It contains many family time ideas to help with meaningful, Bible-centered worship. Write to Gospel Light, 2300 Knoll Drive, Ventura, CA 93003.

• Spend a few sessions reviewing the makeup of the Bible. Talk about how all sixty-six books fit together. There are many good visualized books on this subject. One of the best for elementary school children is *The Bible, God's Wonderful Book* (Bible Club Movement). For adult study before the discussions, *How We Got the Bible* by Neil Lightfoot (Baker), is an excellent book.

• Make up your own Bible quiz or pick up a book of quizzes. Christian bookstores carry many on various subjects and graded for all ages.

• Purchase a book of choral readings from a Christian bookstore and use it occasionally. Standard Press publishes an excellent one titled, *A Year of Choral Readings.*

• Spend several worship times discovering and learning how to use reference materials. Commentaries, concordances, Bible dictionaries and atlases are all valuable Bible study tools. Many are available in easy-to-use-and-understand children's versions. Show how each is used and the type of information it contains. Then make assignments to be shared at later worship times.

• Write individual or group poetry. One family uses the best of these for homemade Christmas and birthday cards.

• Study the Lord's Prayer, the Beatitudes or the 23rd Psalm. Children love to participate by making a scrapbook of pictures illustrating the passage.

• Let little ones have the regular responsibility of laying out the materials required for family worship.

• Tell about the person you had the most fun with today. Why do you think God allowed that person to be near you today? Read the story of Jonathan and David (I Samuel 18, 19 and 20).

• Tell what you like about your family. Read Deuteronomy 6:1,2,5-9; Proverbs 1:7-9; 22:6; and Ephesians 6:1-4. Then praise God for the love, health and unity of your family.

• Discuss how the Bible has helped you lately.

• Discuss what God is like and how we know about Him. Read Psalm 139, and Job 37, 38 and 39.

• Talk and pray about specific or pseudo-situations. For instance:

What shall we do about the neighbor's dog tromping down our garden?

How should Mary Jo handle her low math grade when she thinks she deserves a higher one?

If you knew your best friend was stealing, what would you do?

If you saw marijuana being passed around at school, what would you do and why?

There is a mute, paralyzed person in the nursing home. How can we communicate and show our love?

Is war ever right?

How much should our family give to the church? Should we give to other organizations too?

What about the neighbor kids who misuse toys?

What can we say to the children next-door whose parents are divorcing?

• **Make worship times around certain events extra special. Work in your own family traditions or use some of these ideas:**

For *Christmas,* small children will love baking a birthday cake for Jesus. One grandmother joined the celebration by phoning a bakery long distance and ordering a cake. She sent Christmas plates, cups and napkins in the mail. The family sang carols, read the Christmas story, lit the candle in the middle of the cake, and sang "Happy Birthday" to Jesus.

For *New Year's Eve,* read Psalm 90:1-14 and 102:24-27. Sing "Another Year Is Dawning." Pass a "cup of blessing" around the table, each taking a sip from the common vessel and telling the best thing God brought into his life the past year. Sit in front of a glowing fireplace. Let the kids stay up as late as they can and hold the celebration as near midnight as possible. Share the happiest day of the year, the most disappointing, and the most satisfying. Afterward, light candles from the fireplace and sing "Blest Be the Tie that Binds."

For *Easter,* borrow Holy Land slides from your pastor or friends who have been there. Or borrow slides or a filmstrip from your church library. Three filmstrips are available from David C. Cook ("Jesus Enters Jerusalem," "Jesus Goes to Calvary," and "Jesus Is Alive Again"). Plant a tree to signify new life.

For a family member's *baptism,* borrow books or slides that explain its meaning. Read Scripture from Mark 1 or Romans 6. Discuss the baptismal service itself. *New Life for Boys and Girls* (Accent) is excellent follow-up material.

For *birthdays,* staple colored sheets of construction paper to white cardboard and use as placemats. After the meal, ask each family member to draw something nice he would like to have happen in the life of the birthday person.

When your home is touched by the *death* of a close friend or relative, use the family worship time before the funeral to talk about God's marvelous provisions for Christians. Bring an unshelled peanut and use it as an object lesson. Talk about how the inside is more important than the outside (I Samuel 16:7). Compare the empty shell to the empty body in the casket. Help little ones understand that the important part (the "inside" or the soul) is with Jesus; only the empty body is left behind. Use John 14 and I Thessalonians 4:13-18 or I Corinthians 15:51-58 for more in-depth studies.

• One evening worship time, pass out paper and pencils. Have each person write down some good thoughts to begin the next day with when he first opens his eyes. For thought-primers, read aloud Isaiah 40:28-31; Psalm 90:1,2; or Psalm 118:24.

Helpful Books for
Creative Family Worship

Christian Family Activities by Wayne Rickerson (Standard). Two versions: a year's activities for families with children or for families with teens.

Christian Family Activities by Bobbie Reed (Standard). A year's activities for one-parent families.

Devotions, a Family Affair by Ruth M. Ward (Masters Press).

Fun Ideas for Family Devotions with Activity Pages by Ginger Jurries and Karen Mulder (Standard). For families with children ages 5-10 years.

Family Evening Activity Devotions by Ron Brusius and Margaret Noettl (Concordia). Tested devotions for families of all ages, for single parent use or 2-parent families.

Families Sharing God by Gertrude Ann Priester (Westminster). Devotions that answer questions of young children.

Happiness Is a Family Walk with God by Lois Bock and Miji Working (Revell).

Happy Moments with God by Margaret Anderson (Bethany). Devotions for families with young children.

Happy Talk by Annetta E. Dellinger (Concordia). Devotions for families with young children.

Potter and Clay by Muriel Blackwell (Broadman). Prose and poetry to inspire and motivate those working with children.

Special Times with God by David and Naomi Shibley (Nelson). Family devotions with young children.

Wings of Joy by Joan Winmill Brown (Revell). Inspiring quotations, poetry and Scripture passages by topics.

Worship Is for Kids Too by Ruth Ward (Baker).

Materials to Use with Young Children

Answers for Your Child, by Carolyn Nystrom, (Moody Press). Solid answers for questions like, ''What happens when we die?'' and, ''Who is God?''

Benjie Beaver Series by Francis Walter and Violet T. Pearson (Accent Books). Fun-filled adventures of a beaver family illustrate Bible truths.

Bible Lessons for Little People by Evelyn Groggs and Sarah Eberle (Standard).

Bible Rhymes to Say and Do by Ruth Beechich (Accent Books).

Ethel Barrett Tells Favorite Bible Stories (Regal).

Finger Puppets Help Teach by Meredith Goodrich (Accent Books).

First Steps, Bible Stories for Children by Charles Foster (Moody Press).

Jesus, the Friend of Children with illustrations by Richard and Frances Hook (Cook). 49 Bible stories in easy to understand language for children from 4-8 years.

Leading Little Ones to God by Marian M.

Schoolland (Eerdmans). A child's book of Bible doctrinal teachings.

Little Visits with God by Allan Hart Jahsmann and Martin Simon (Concordia). Devotions for families with small children.

Stories for the Children's Hour by Kenneth Taylor (Moody Press). Insights into the behavior Jesus wants with questions and answers after each chapter.

Tell Me About Jesus by Mary Alice Jones (Randy McNally/WHSE). Answers to children's questions.

The Bible in Pictures for Little Eyes by Kenneth Taylor (Moody Press). Early Bible stories depicting the great doctrines of God with pictures for each story for children 3-6 years.

The Best Friend of All by Mary E. LeBar (Victor). A book for ages 6-8 showing how to become God's child and enjoy Him as Heavenly Father.

The Very Best Book of All by Fran Flournoy (Standard). A book about the Bible for very young children.

Books to Use with Juniors

Between You and Me, God by Patricia A. Simmons (Broadman). 72 prayers to help girls 9-12 with problems of growing up.

Creation: for Kids and Other People Too by Judy Stonecipher (Accent Books). Enjoyable poetry which tells the 6-days creation story.

Daily Devotions for Juniors by Ruth I. Johnson

(Moody Press).

Guess What, God! by Patricia A. Simmons (Broadman). 72 prayers to help boys 9-12 talk to God.

Jeff and Jenny Series by Nellie Frisinger (Accent Books). Adventure books about twins who learn to trust God in their exciting pre-teen years.

Learning the Books of the New Testament by Marilyn B. Cox (Broadman). Programmed instruction with blanks to fill in.

Tell Us a Story by Julius Fischback (Broadman). A wide range of subject matter: great Bible personalities, attitudes, special days, things from nature.

Can You Tell Me? by Dena Korfker (Zondervan). Answers 39 important questions your child is sure to ask about God and the faith.

Books to Use with Teens

Bernard Palmer Series (Accent Books). For young teens; titles include *Case of the Missing Dinosaur, Clue of the Old Sea Chest, Mystery at Poor Boy's Folly, Rebel of the Lazy H Ranch.*

Escape by Rachel Martin as told to Bonnie Palmer Young (Accent Books). A young woman's account of being duped into following a cult leader and of her rescue from that cult.

Found: God's Will by John MacArthur Jr.

(Scripture Press). A logical and Biblical discussion of how to find God's will for one's life.

Fully Alive by Gloria Gage (Accent Books). The true story of a Christian high schooler whose football career was ended by cancer. Inspiring reading about the faith of this young man.

Just Between God and Me by Sandra Drescher (Scripture Press). Daily devotions for college age persons.

Mountain Trailways for Youth by Mrs. Charles Cowman (Zondervan). A daily devotional book that talks the language and understands problems of young people.

Search for the Avenger by Lee Roddy (Accent Books). Hawaiian adventure and intrigue for youthful readers.

That's a Good Question by Roger Forster and V. Paul Marston (Tyndale). Reasonable answers about a living faith.

Teen Talks With God by Robert Boden (Concordia)

The Restless Summer by Nina Walje (Accent Books). A story of teenage love and rebellion, with Scriptural principles for teens to follow.

Other:

Campus Life magazine, Box 419, Wheaton, IL 60187: a magazine for teens featuring a fun format with deep truths interspersed.

Books for Parents

Helping Your Child Discover Faith by Delia T. Halverson (Judson).

Teaching Your Child About God by Wesley Haystead (Regal).

Train Up a Child and Be Glad You Did by Harold J. Sala (Accent Books). Practical tips for successful child rearing.

When Parents Cry by Joy P. Gage (Accent Books). Help for parents who are trying to cope with teenage rebellion.

Other:

Evangelizing Today's Child, a magazine published by Child Evangelism Fellowship, Morrison, CO 80465. Its purpose is to equip Christians to win children to Christ and disciple them; includes children's stories, quizzes, visualized lessons, teaching tips.

Family Walk, P. O. Box 80587, Atlanta, GA 30366. A magazine with ideas for stimulating family discussion on meaningful subjects.

Chapter 4

A Child's Personal Decision

for Christ

Jesus said, "Let the children alone, and do not hinder them from coming to Me; for the kingdom of heaven belongs to such as these."

—Matthew 19:14

Some parents assume their child is a Christian when it is not so. A child must make a personal decision for Christ. He must be told that eternal life is not inherited from his parents and that there are no second generation Christians.

I have met only five mothers over the years who have personally led their own children to the Lord! Even in strong Bible-centered homes, parents sometimes skirt the issue with embarrassment. They seem to depend on the church to challenge their children to make a definite decision. Most people who do not accept Christ when they are children or young people, never do so at all. The older people grow, the more difficult the decision becomes. Surely the children of believers ought to be believers too!

No parent has a right to rest until each youngster has made a commitment to the Lord. It is a high calling to lead a child from spiritual blindness into the Light. It is a thrill to see a child possess with surety his title as a chosen person, adopted into God's family, planned for since God created the world and loved as much as the Son of God Himself. Lead your child early to take his crown and claim his citizenship in the kingdom of God. Teach him that possession is firm because Christ is holding on to him. Assure him that he is linked inseparably and eternally to God by his steadfast decision to follow Jesus.

Why Lead Children to Christ?

Perhaps the key to fighting juvenile delinquency is the salvation of children before adolescence for this is when Satan wars so mightily and successfully in their ranks. Once the job of evangelizing is done, and the child's decision is made, the Holy Spirit will begin to direct the young life. Our God is the God of children too, and will do far more than we ask or think. He provides an added measure of help through times of temptation and trouble. A Christian child has at least some self-discipline and restraint from sin. And if by adolescence, he has had several years of training for Christ, he is more likely to make better decisions about his life and more choices that will honor God. The Holy Spirit living inside a youngster is not only a powerful leveler for that young person, but also a source of hope for frustrated parents.

It is pathetic to hear moms and dads crying out to God, in tears, for the salvation of disobedient teens. It would have been much easier to bring them to Christ earlier, and that would have allowed years at home for nurture of their faith. It is interesting to theorize that the world would not have to endure permissiveness, disrespect for authority and irreverence for Almighty God if all parents led their offspring to Christ early and trained them well in the Word.

Presenting the gospel to children is significant business. We are dealing with human beings, not "just children." The conversion of an adult is no more important. Children have great potential to influence the world. God is watching. So are angels. And it is awesome to think that sharing with youngsters is God's way of putting His plan into operation. It is God's way of insuring that the children entrusted to us pass from spiritual death into new life in Christ. Long after contemporary buildings crumble and monuments erode, a child with his unlimited capabilities can be persuading others to believe. And it just may be that the door to bringing the world to its knees before Almighty God is through child evangelism.

Who Can Lead a Child to Christ?

Almost anyone. It is far easier to approach youngsters with the gospel than adults. Kids are not nearly so critical. And kids are almost always willing to listen. They do not expect big words or high-powered knowledge, and they will respond positively more often than not.

What are the qualifications for sharing Christ with children? The purveyor of the gospel must be born again. He must have patience, a desire and a method of sharing the Word. He must have a proper attitude, counting it a privilege to be an instrument of God. He must be utterly dependent on the Holy Spirit to convict and convince the child of the truth.

As a Christian parent, you can claim your children for the Lord years ahead of their actual salvation experience. You can pray ceaselessly for God's power on behalf of your youngsters and their decisions for God. We do not work alone. As God's sons and daughters, we born-again moms and dads have the Holy Spirit's wisdom, power and love so we can lead our kids to Christ. We can approach the subject of salvation with great surety and confidence, knowing the Holy Spirit will help us find just the right words to say. Remember that ultimately youngsters belong to Him, are returnable to Him, and that the Spirit's interest in seeing them saved is enormous. He will apply the truth of Scripture and open their minds to see the Savior. And He is the one who sets the timetable for conversion. This knowledge takes the pressure off the parent to press for a decision "today." As Bill Bright, president of Campus Crusade for Christ says, "We share Christ in the power of the Holy Spirit and leave the results to God." We can trust the Holy Spirit's timing. If a child is not ready, the parent's job is to try again later, and perhaps even again, until the youngster fully understands and willingly accepts the claims of Christ upon his life.

The exciting fact is that when the job is done, we parents have then reproduced baby Christians! We need not necessarily go to the mission field for our converts. Through spiritual multiplication, our saved children sharing with *their* children could make us spiritual grandparents — or even great-grandparents before we die!

When Can a Child Be Led to Christ?

You can block a child's way to God by delaying his salvation. There is no place in the Bible that sets an appropriate age. Normally, a child is perfectly able to understand the gospel story at a very young age and should not be denied the truths of God. Our school systems would have us believe that six years of age is the right time to begin formal teaching of children, and that there is a correct age to introduce every item thereafter. Some say there is an "age of accountability" when a child knows right from wrong, and some have speculated that age is between eleven and thirteen years. Others believe a small youngster does not have the intelligence or wisdom to understand what accepting Christ means.

But do not be timid about presenting Christ early! Believing Christ for salvation should not be hard at all. The message of the gospel is simple. Kids understand love, so they understand Jesus. A child doesn't have to be very old to recognize and say, "God loves me." The message of John 3:16 can be comprehended by even a five-year-old. Children respond to love, and they too can see that giving up one's life for another is the highest form of caring. But there is more to salvation than realizing that "God is love." The child must also realize that he is a sinner, that sin is awful in God's sight, and that Jesus died for his sins. When a child can grasp those facts, he may then be ready to be saved.

Entrance into God's kingdom is child-sized

and does not depend on a wealth of wisdom, money or anything else children do not have. Salvation is believing, and a child in his unsophisticated world has more faith than many adults. Most children trust nearly everyone, so it is easy for them to trust Christ. There are no great theological depths to be explored and understood. Only a kid-sized bit of information is needed to be saved. Even adults have to be saved on children's terms, coming with a simple understanding and faith. Why, then, do we question that a child can come to Christ? That simple childlikeness is not a deterrent, but a natural channel to God for youngsters.

The new birth often occurs in the lives of six- or eight-year-olds. Many missionaries, pastors and strong laymen became believers at a very early age. Believing does not require an adult mind and we have no right to discourage a decision at any age.

After salvation, a child learns more and more about what he has done. His faith grows as the years go by. In Vacation Bible School one summer, I taught the first graders a simple five-minute lesson on salvation and told the children they would need to make a decision about Christ someday. I quietly asked that anyone ready now, let me know privately afterward. One seven-year-old told me firmly that she had already prayed and received Christ into her life. She was absolutely sure.

If we tell our kids from the time they are very

small that God is love, that Jesus died for them, and that believers belong to God, then it is perfectly natural to expect that they will be saved — possibly before the age of twelve. Didn't we dole out the gospel carefully in bedtime stories hoping for just that? Then why hinder a child's decision when he is ready? Let him come at the time of life when it is easiest of all. And when he makes that decision, accept it as real. Our children's salvation should not arouse our suspicions. We should not doubt the authenticity of their response. They are the natural fruits of our teaching and the Holy Spirit's promised work.

Encourage the young believer. Show him the assurance of his salvation. Use John 3:36; 6:37; 10:28; 2 Timothy 1:12; Titus 1:2; and I John 5:11-13. And tell him, "Yes, if you believe that you have sinned, and that Jesus died and rose again, you are saved forever. And no matter what else happens, when you die, you will go to live in Heaven."

No Pushing, Please

Watch for your child's readiness. Avoid manipulative techniques. And never press children to walk the church aisles. Some kids will "go forward" during an invitation at church just to gain attention or to do what they think is expected. Any human juggling apart for the Holy Spirit's influence accomplishes little.

Some youngsters can apply the plan of salvation faster than others — even in the same family. You may faithfully lay a planned foundation of several years before a child seems ready to make a profession of faith. Or your child may need very little prompting before deciding to follow Christ. The parent's job is to present the claims of Christ clearly and often; directing, not driving the child to Christ. And remember, children are not necessarily saved in the same order they were born. Younger children may receive Christ before older ones.

Matthew 13 tells the story of the sower of seeds. Some seeds fell on good ground, some in stony or thorny places. Children, with their accepting attitudes, are often the "good ground." But if they are not, don't get frantic. Present the gospel again a little bit later. Don't push. Try to remember that as a parent, you are simply the instrument for getting the message to the youngster at your knee. The Holy Spirit is responsible for the timing and results.

What Must a Child Do to Be Saved?

God does not dole out a child-type conversion to people under twelve and another for adults. It is the same message and the same process for both. The child believes in exactly the same way as the adult. There are no tryout periods and no special concessions for the young. The gospel is simple enough for all to comprehend: All — men, women and children have sinned, and Jesus died for each.

It is important not to talk down to the youngster. You are after a vital decision. Once you have prepared the way with the basic story, invite the child to accept Christ. It is easy to simply tell the story and stop. But that will not get the job done. God wants each little person you deal with to turn to Him. Tell the youngster that just knowing the facts is not enough and ask him to tell you his decision aloud. That will not be hard. Kids respond easily: ''Do you believe all of this, Sue? Then let's pray and invite Christ into your life right now. Do you want to?''

I chose a Saturday when it was pouring rain to share with one of our daughters. To me, there is hidden beauty in rain splashing against windows and running fervently through the eaves. A dark day provides opportunity to enjoy indoor things. There was no chance little friends would knock on the door; there was nothing much on afternoon TV to intrigue her; and there was certainly no lure to go out and play since water overflowed the street curbs. Plainly, there was not much of anything to do. So Mary Jo listened attentively.

Once in a while a child will come to you and ask how to become a Christian. Perhaps a special Sunday school lesson or a book or message will prompt the question. More often, however, the parent will need to take the initiative. You could write a letter to the child as I did and post it on his bedroom door:

> Big doings at 4 p.m. in my room. Cookies and milk and important talk. Meet me there today.
>
> Love,
>
> Mom

Or you might say, "Let's sit together by ourselves in the den (porch swing, hammock). I have something important to talk to you about."

If you're not exactly sure how to begin the "important talk," try ordering the pamphlet, *Good News* (Campus Crusade for Christ). Read it together with your child. This pamphlet is one of the best ways to share the gospel. Each booklet has a place where the youngster can fill his name in John 3:16 to personalize what Christ has done for him. Afterward, you might want to send for the follow-up materials offered on the inside back cover. Or order free children's beginner Bible correspondence courses from Billy Graham, Minneapolis, MN 55403; or from Mailbox Bible Club, Upper Darby, PA 19082.

Scripture Press publishes an 11 x 17 inch visualized chart titled, "How to Become God's Child." It explains in primary-age language what happens when a child receives Jesus and how to live as a member of God's family.

Bible Club distributes a short tract, "A Child

of God," which is also an excellent gospel challenge for children as does Grace Gospel Fellowship, Inc., P.O. Box 97, San Dimas, CA 91773.

What Now that the Child Has Received Christ?

Pray for the child relentlessly. Prayer is a parent's secret service on behalf of a youngster. Depend on the Spirit to work daily. And encourage the child to tell others about his decision to follow Christ. Telling others will reinforce in his own mind that something important has happened. Go over the plan of salvation again and tell him he can share Christ with someone else just as you shared with him.

Nurture discipleship. Help your child to adopt an attitude of, "Okay, Lord, what do You want of me? I want to follow You; You are my leader."

Reinforce his assurance of salvation: "No matter how you feel, you can trust God's Word and what it says. You don't have to *feel* saved. God's Word says you belong to God because you believe Christ died for you. And whatever God's Word says is true. Some mornings you may wake up feeling really 'blah.' You may not *feel* saved. You may feel like God has disappeared. But you are still God's child on those days, too. And God never disappears. He said He would never leave. Believe it."

A child's assurance of salvation usually comes easier than an adult's. The simple childlike faith that brought him to God also swings into action when extra faith is needed. Most kids just believe they are God's and that is that. They seem to have uncomplicated assurance of what God has done in their lives.

But what if a child wants to ask Christ into his life a second time? Don't panic. Reaffirm that once is enough. God keeps His promises. Read John 3:36; 6:37; 10:28; 2 Timothy 1:12; Titus 1:2; and I John 5:11-13. If you wish you can then say, "Let's make it final once and for all right now, asking Christ in forever. Then you will never have to do it again."

Above all, be very much aware of the infinite value of the child you are dealing with and the decision he has made. A child's salvation can be very real indeed and is of immeasurable worth, unfathomably important. God allows kids into His family and we need to welcome them in also. An immortal spirit has determined its eternal destiny. A human being has begun to love the Lord with all his heart, soul and mind. Spiritual beginnings are often frail and tender, but nonetheless valid and wonderful. Encourage the child in the faith by smiling on what he has done. And let him know you respect his decision as real.

Don't expect perfect behavior because of the youngster's conversion. Remember, only simple faith is needed to come to Christ (Ephesians 2:8,9; Acts 16:31). Immediate conduct is not required. Although a child of God is a new person (2 Corinthians 5:17), he needs time to grow. Help him by allowing for some miserable stumbling and willful disobedience. And recognize each wonderful success along his Christian learning process.

A friend of mine tells the story of a shipboard captain who was retiring. For twenty-five years the men had respected his strictness and rigid authority, saluting every time they met him on deck. When he retired, a new captain came aboard, but the former captain remained a while to break him in. Despite the arrival of the new captain, the men sometimes found themselves saluting the old leader out of habit, even though they were beginning to respect the authority of the new. Breaking away from the old captain proved difficult and took time. Just so, when the new authority (the Holy Spirit) arrives in a new Christian's life, He must live side by side with the old nature. It takes a while before the new captain commands respect and obedience. But little by little the signs of growth will appear.

Books to Help Introduce a Child to Christ

Children and Conversion by Clifford Ingle (Broadman).

Counseling Children about Christian Conversion by Daryl Heath (The Sunday School Board).

Explaining Salvation to Children by Marjorie Sonderholm (HIS International Service).

How to Lead Young Children to Christ by William W. Orr (Scripture Press).

Introducing Young Children to Jesus by Violet Meade (SCM Press, London).

Kids and the Kingdom by John Inchley (Tyndale).

Living in God's Family by Mary B. LeBar (Scripture Press).

Salvation, Then What? by Marjorie Sonderholm (HIS International Service).

Tell Me About Becoming a Christian by Derek Prime (Moody Press).

What Can a Child Believe? by Eugene Chamberlain (Broadman).

You Can't Begin Too Soon by Wesley Haystead (Gospel Light Publications).

Chapter 5

When to Teach What

"To whom would He teach knowledge? And to whom would He interpret the message? Those just weaned from milk? Those just taken from the breast?

"For He says, 'Order on order, order on order, Line on line, line on line, A little here, a little there.' "

—Isaiah 28:9, 10

Kids. They are filled with super energy, abounding in unlimited potential for absorbing new ideas about God. Making God's treasures available at just the right times in a child's life will build a solid foundation for Christian growth and experience.

Introducing abstract subjects like the meaning of baptism and communion will certainly not harm a child. Like saluting the flag, the

97

young child at first will not fully appreciate the symbolism involved, but he will at least become familiar with the terminology and with the symbol itself. Later on, his understanding will grow and the true meaning will unfold. But too much too soon can cause confusion in the child and disappointment in his teacher. And a very young child subjected to a battery of vague symbolic concepts may see religion as boring or incomprehensible. He may even form incorrect concrete notions that will need to be corrected and relearned at a later date. (For years I connected communion with lunch and magic with Christ's being everywhere.)

But the right ideas introduced at the right times will have far greater impact and will lay a better groundwork, enabling a child to have continuing exciting experiences with God.

That is the purpose of this chapter. It shows when to introduce what and is offered with the hope that moms and dads and teachers will use it with great sensitivity to the Holy Spirit's leading.

The following list of ideas has been gathered from a number of sources through my years of studying, teaching, speaking and parenting. I wish I could remember all those who helped me compile this list so I could give them proper credit, but at this point I must be content with a public expression of appreciation to each one. Thank you.

Now, please keep in mind that this chart serves only as a guideline; each youngster develops at his own speed, some comprehending difficult concepts earlier than others. You know your child better than anybody else. When you know he is ready, teach!

15 Months to 3 Years

Characteristics:

Short attention span.

Likes playing alone.

Cannot form concepts.

Quite restless.

Is best taught alone, one-on-one, in brief sessions.

Loves to be read to; loves pictures.
Try *Bible Pictures* and *First Steps for Little Feet* by Charles Foster (Moody Press).

Loves to be rocked and sung to.

Can Learn These Bible Truths:

Children should obey their parents.

We go to church to learn about God.

God watches over me.

God made the world.

The Bible tells about God.

God loves me.

Can Master These Skills:

Saying a short prayer.

Singing.
Teach "Jesus Loves Me" and "Away In a Manger."

——————————**4 and 5 Years**——————————

Characteristics:

Very inquisitive.

Full of energy.

Growing fast.

Believes everything.

Loves to hear favorite stories over and over.

Loves Jesus stories.

Enjoys Sunday school usually.

Sees mother as a very important person.

Can Learn These Bible Truths:

Jesus died for sin.

Jesus never leaves me.

God made everything.

God loves children.

God wants children to obey their parents.

God wants children to be kind and to share.

The Bible is important because it tells what God
wants us to know.

Can Master This Skill:

Learning short verses by casual repetition.
(The word "memorize" is not understood yet.)

——————————**6 to 8 Years**——————————

Characteristics:

Curious and active.

Needs to be kept busy.

Terrific imagination.

Believes most of what he is told.

Developing sense of right and wrong.

Usually wants to please parents.

Sensitive to approval or disapproval.

Less self-centered now; developing some concern for others.

Doing things with others more important now.

Usually not ready to learn abstract concepts.

Can usually read some, even a little from the Bible with help.

Prays, trying to get God to do things, regardless of His will.

Loves interesting stories of Bible people.
> Teach the lives of Jesus, Zaccheus, the Good Samaritan, Samuel, Eli, David.

Can Learn:

The Bible is true.

God is the Creator.

God sees all and is a powerful helper.

God loves everyone.

Jesus is the Son of God, Jesus was born, died, rose again and is in Heaven.

Everyone sins and God is the only One who can forgive sin.

Everyone needs to accept Jesus as Savior.
> (A few children will be ready to invite Christ into their lives at this age.)

The Church is made up of people who believe in Jesus.

Heaven is for people who accept Jesus.

Satan is glad when people sin.
> (For extra help, use *Devotions for the Children's Hour* by Kenneth Taylor (Moody Press) or *Leading Little Ones to God* by Marian M. Schoolland (William Eerdmans).

Can Master These Skills:

Using the Bible some.

Beginning to learn the books of the Old and New Testaments.

Memorizing passages of Scripture like the 23rd Psalm and the Lord's Prayer.

——————9 to 12 Years ——————

Characteristics:

Beginning to talk about his faith now.

Applying truths gives some trouble.

Likes to discover through research and learn new things.

Attention span good.

Slowing some in physical growth.

Has great energy; loves to be on the move.

Peer pressure growing.

Likes working in groups.

Often loud, competitive.

Often likes history.

Will often copy heroes from character/action stories.

Can Learn These Bible Truths:

How the Bible came to us and its flawless character.

God has a purpose for everyone's life.

Prayer is powerful.

God is majestic, awesome, holy.

The meanings of parables and other symbolic concepts in the Bible.

How the local church functions and the jobs of its staff.

About what other denominations believe, the danger of cults.

Can Master These Skills:

Bible study.

Giving.

Witnessing.

Putting some Christian service principles into action.

─────────13 to 16 Years ─────────

Characteristics:

Peer pressure very great.

Growing independent of parents.

Thinking about a vocation.

Abstract thinking now possible.

Religious ideas may waver from radical to rigid with great emotion.

May question God.

May come up with beliefs different from parents.

Each develops physically, spiritually and emotionally more diversely from others than in earlier years; each sets his own individualized pace.

Matures very fast; girls mature faster than boys.

Home activities become less important; outside activities more important.

Needs love, understanding, sympathy and stabilizing influence.

Tries to understand life and develop an identity.

Spends a lot of time thinking about God, life, death and the "why's" of life.

Understands what ethics are.

Can Learn These Bible Truths:

The reliability of the Bible.

The dependable, unchangeable, inalterable character of Jesus.

The will of God.

The ministries of the Holy Spirit.
(helper, guide, teacher, comforter, etc.)

How to receive Christ personally and to share that faith with others.

Church doctrines and their meanings.

Church history, new movements in Christianity.

Can Master These Skills:

Bible study.

Lifestyle.

Career.

Using reference materials and methods of all types.

Chapter 6

At Home... Ten Minutes a Day

"Give us this day our daily bread."
—Jesus, in Matthew 6:11

It does not take great knowledge of Scripture to lead children into the Bible and along the doctrinal path. Soft organ music, stained glass windows, well-equipped Sunday school rooms and long lectures are not required. All it takes is a concerned adult with a plan and determination. Some parents feel so inadequate that they avoid home Bible teaching. But there are no perfect parents to pass on the faith — only us — imperfect and sinful as we are. God has used people just like us to preserve His divine rule ever since the days of Adam and Eve. We, then, must accept our responsibility to further preserve it by passing it on to our children and grandchildren.

This last chapter is designed to produce people with a faith stronger than that of the generation before: children better than ourselves. The simple strategy can begin at about age nine and requires only two to ten minutes daily. Just a short time each day is an invaluable investment in rock-like spiritual underpinnings to sustain the future adult for life. There is no teacher's manual. The Bible itself is the only tool. But moms and dads will be learning too, because every contact with the Word will help them as well as the kids.

An easy to understand paraphrase of the Bible might be particularly appropriate for your child, and the one I recommend is The Living Bible, published by Tyndale House Publishers of Wheaton,, Illinois.

Here's how the plan works: Read a short passage each night. Scriptures are arranged topically. Each theme will be covered in depth, in some cases for two months. Each week, one verse is highlighted for nightly review and memorization if desired.

With this program, you and your youngster will read large portions of the Bible together. In one year, you will focus in detail on fifty-two verses. Little preparation is required because no comments are needed unless you desire to make some. The Bible readings can speak for themselves, and the Holy Spirit can do the teaching. (John 16:13).

Using this simple plan, your child can have daily contact with God's Word under a personal tutor. He can develop a feel for the language of the Bible and begin to understand its makeup early in life so he is "at home" reading and studying it. Children will quickly learn the location of various books and how to locate specific references by handling the Bible nightly. And they will gain respect for the Bible as an authoritative source, seeing it as an instruction book for living, given by God Himself. Kids will learn early that the search for God's truth begins and ends in the Bible.

This approach is portable and its concepts transferable. Moving down the block, out of state or even going on vacation will make no difference in the nightly routine. The youngster's instruction can easily continue. His steady diet of one-topic Bible readings can go right on. Verses for emphasis can be put on cards and taken along. They can be posted on the dashboard, or on the motel room's desk for convenient and casual review. And weekly verses can be shortened or lengthened according to a child's age and ability.

Here are fifteen months of nightly readings to get started. When these are completed, any parent using a concordance can easily compile more topical listings. After two or three years the assignments can be repeated for valuable review.

15 Months of Nightly Readings

Scripture Reading	*Memory Verse*
The Bible: Why Was It Written?	Hebrews 4:12

1. John 20:30,31
2. Psalm 19:7-11
3. I Timothy 3:14-17
4. Hebrews 4:12
   Proverbs 1:33
5. Psalm 119:9,10
6. Psalm 119:96-105
7. Deuteronomy 17:18-20

---

2 Timothy 3:16

1. Matthew 4:4
   Romans 1:16,17
2. 1 Peter 2:2-4
3. John 5:39
4. Romans 10:9-13
5. Revelation 1:1-3
6. James 1:21-25
7. John 15:1-3

Psalm 119:105

1. Isaiah 55:8-13
2. Ephesians 6:13-18
3. 1 John 5:13
4. 2 Peter 1:19-21
5. 1 Peter 1:10-13
6. 1 Peter 1:23-25

The Bible: Its Writers and How They Viewed Their Jobs:

7. Amos 7:14-16

15 Months of Nightly Readings

Scripture Reading	*Memory Verse*

1. 2 Samuel 23:1,2   2 Peter 1:20,21
2. Jeremiah 1:4-10
3. Ezekiel 3:1-11
Understanding the Bible; Wisdom:
4. 1 Corinthians 2:14-16
5. John 14:15-17,26 (The Holy Spirit is the key)
6. John 16:13
7. 1 John 2:20b,27

---

1. 1 Corinthians 2:7-10   Psalm 119:11
2. 1 Corinthians 2:11-13
3. Psalm 119:11
4. Psalm 119:12-17
5. Psalm 119:18,19
6. James 1:5b-8
7. Psalm 25:14

Prayer: Psalm 34:15
1. Psalm 11:4,7
2. Psalm 34:15,17
3. Psalm 66:18
4. Psalm 130:1-6
5. Proverbs 28:9
6. 1 John 3:19-22
7. Isaiah 58:1-9

---

15 Months of Nightly Readings

Scripture Reading	Memory Verse

1. Isaiah 59:1-9 — Psalm 66:18
2. John 15:7-17
3. Mark 11:24,25
4. 1 Peter 3:7-12
How to pray:
5. Ephesians 6:18-20
6. Luke 11:5-10
7. Matthew 6:5-15

---

1. Matthew 21:16 — Colossians 4:2
2. Colossians 4:2
   Philippians 4:6,7
3. 1 Samuel 12:23
   1 Timothy 2:1-3
4. John 16:22-26
5. Hebrews 4:13-16
6. Jude 20
7. Luke 18:1-14

Prayer: Does it Work? — John 15:7
1. John 14:12-14
2. Acts 12:1-11
3. Psalm 4:3
4. Psalm 86:5-7
5. Psalm 91:14,15
6. Psalm 34:3,4
7. Psalm 55:16-18

15 Months of Nightly Readings

Scripture Reading	*Memory Verse*
1. Matthew 21:22	James 5:16b
2. John 15:5-7	
3. 1 John 5:12-15	
4. James 5:13-18	
5. Romans 8:15,16,26,27	
6. Colossians 2:1,2	
7. Daniel 6:3-10	

1. Mark 14:32-39	Psalm 4:4
2. Luke 5:15,16	
3. Joshua 10:13,14	
4. Mark 1:35 (Jesus prayed.)	
5. Mark 9:25-29	
6. 2 Corinthians 1:9-11	
7. Psalm 4:1-4	

How to Pray:	Matthew 5:44
1. Matthew 5:44-48 Proverbs 29:10 (Pray for enemies.)	
2. Matthew 6:10,11 (Pray for God's will to be done; for daily food.)	
3. Matthew 6:12,13 (Pray for forgiveness; deliverance from evil.)	

15 Months of Nightly Readings

Scripture Reading   *Memory Verse*

4. Luke 22:40
   Mark 14:38 (Pray
   you enter not into
   temptation.)
5. Ezra 6:10
6. James 5:15,16 (Pray
   for the sick.)
7. Romans 10:1 (Pray
   for unbelievers.)

1. Ephesians 1:16-23   Ephesians 1:18,19
2. 2 Samuel 7:27
   Matthew 11:25
3. Jeremiah 33:3
   James 5:17,18
4. James 5:13
5. 1 John 5:16
6. Matthew 9:38
7. 2 Chronicles 7:14
   Ephesians 6:19

If You Feel Worried: Matthew 6:34
1. Proverbs 3:4-6
2. Psalm 55:17-19,22
3. Proverbs 20:24
   Psalm 124:8
4. Psalm 125:1,2
5. Matthew 6:25-34
6. Psalm 18:2,3
7. Psalm 18:30-36

15 Months of Nightly Readings

Scripture Reading	*Memory Verse*
1. Isaiah 41:10,13	Isaiah 41:13
2. Luke 12:25	
3. Hebrews 13:6b,8	
4. Psalm 23	
5. Psalm 33:13-22	
6. Mark 4:35-41	
7. Psalm 121:1-8	

1. Philippians 4:6,7	Philippians 4:6,7
2. 1 John 4:16a,18	
3. Psalm 59:9, 10a,16,17	
4. Psalm 27:1-6	
5. Psalm 27:14	
6. Psalm 56:3,8-12	
7. Luke 6:47,48	

1. Psalm 118:1,4,6	Psalm 118:6
2. Proverbs 19:23	
If You feel all alone:	
3. Psalm 54:4 Psalm 14:5b	
4. Revelation 3:20	
5. Matthew 28:20b	
6. Joshua 1:9 Ephesians 3:12	
7. 1 Peter 1:2	

1. Matthew 10:29-31	Matthew 10:29,31
2. Ephesians 2:9-13	

15 Months of Nightly Readings

Scripture Reading	*Memory Verse*
3. Ephesians 2:18-22	
4. 1 Peter 2:9b,10	
5. Romans 8:14-16	
6. John 1:1-13	
7. John 14:15-19	

1. John 16:27	Ephesians 3:17b-19a
2. Colossians 1:20-23	
3. Ephesians 3:17-21	
4. John 3:15,16	
5. 1 Corinthians 2:9	
6. Romans 8:35-39	
7. Romans 8:35-39	
(repeat)	

1. 1 Peter 5:7	1 Peter 5:7
2. Psalm 48:14	
Psalm 32:8	
3. 1 Chronicles 16:9	
4. Ephesians 1:4,5	
5. Hebrews 4:13	
He protects you:	
6. Proverbs 3:25	
Psalm 32:7	
7. Psalm 9:1-11	

If You Feel Discouraged:	Isaiah 43:2a,3a
1. Psalm 42:1-11	
2. Psalm 130:1-7	
3. Psalm 31:2-12,19-21	

15 Months of Nightly Readings

Scripture Reading	*Memory Verse*
4. Jeremiah 20:11-18	
5. Psalm 102:1-7	
6. 1 Peter 5:7-11	
7. Psalm 43:1-3	
Ephesians 1:8	

1. 2 Corinthians 1:3-5	Romans 8:28
Romans 8:28	
2. Romans 15:13	
1 Corinthians 2:9	
3. Psalm 147:5,6	
4. Philippians 4:4-7	
5. Psalm 34:17-19	
6. Exodus 2:23-25	
Isaiah 49:13-15	
7. Psalm 40:1-4	
John 14:18	

Is Jesus God?	John 1:1
1. Colossians 1:15,16	
2. Colossians 1:17	
3. John 1:1-3	
4. 1 Peter 2:22-25	
5. Mark 1:22	
6. 1 Timothy 3:16	
7. Matthew 3:13-17	

1. Matthew 17:1-8	Matthew 17:5b
2. Acts 3:11-15	
3. 1 Peter 1:18-21	

15 Months of Nightly Readings

Scripture Reading	Memory Verse
4. 1 Peter 3:22	
5. Matthew 16:15,16	
6. 2 Peter 1:16-18	
7. 1 Peter 1:19,20	
Mark 15:33-39	

Scripture Reading	Memory Verse
1. Matthew 27:31,46-53	I Peter 2:22,23
2. Matthew 14:23-33	
3. John 1:10-12	
4. John 1:18	
5. John 1:32-36	
6. John 3:33-36	
7. John 20:20-29	
Luke 7:11-23	

Scripture Reading	Memory Verse
1. 1 John 5:8b	John 14:6
2. John 3:9-18 (What Jesus said about Himself.)	
3. John 7:11-18	
4. Matthew 26:63b,64	
5. Matthew 27:11	
6. John 8:12-16	
7. John 8:53-58	

Scripture Reading	Memory Verse
1. John 14:6-11	John 8:12b
2. John 17:24-26	
3. John 2:13-16	
4. Matthew 11:27	

15 Months of Nightly Readings

Scripture Reading	*Memory Verse*

5. Luke 10:21,22
   John 10:30-33
6. Matthew 28:20b
7. Mark 14:61,62
   Matthew 16:16,17
   (How Christ
   responded to Peter's
   calling Him God.)

Jesus Fulfilled Prophecy:	Micah 5:2

1. Micah 5:2-5
   Matthew 2:3-12
2. Isaiah 9:1,2
   John 8:12b
3. Isaiah 9:1,2
   Matthew 4:12-15
4. Matthew 12:14-21
5. Matthew 26:52-56
6. Acts 2:1-21
7. Isaiah 53:2-10
   (repeat)
   1 Peter 2:21-25

	Isaiah 7:14

1. Isaiah 7:14
2. Matthew 1:18,22,23
   (fulfillment of Isaiah
   7:14)
3. Micah 5:2
4. Luke 2:4,6,7 (fulfill-
   ment of Micah 5:2)

15 Months of Nightly Readings

Scripture Reading	*Memory Verse*
5. Psalm 16:10 Acts 2:31,32 (fulfill- ment of Psalm 16:10) 6. Psalm 22:14-18,22 7. Matthew 27:35 (fulfillment of Psalm 22)	

1. Acts 2:22-32	Acts 2:22
2. Mark 15:22-24	
3. Psalm 22:18 (fulfill- ment of above)	
4. Mark 14:21	
5. Romans 1:1-4	
Miracles Prove Jesus Is God:	
6. Acts 2:22	
7. Mark 16:20	

1. Mark 5:1-20	Mark 6:56b
2. Mark 5:25-34	
3. Mark 5:35-43	
4. Mark 6:30-44	
5. Mark 6:46-56	
6. John 5:2-9b	
7. John 5:14,15,31-40	

1. John 10:22-42	John 10:30
2. Matthew 8:14-17	

15 Months of Nightly Readings

Scripture Reading	*Memory Verse*

3. Matthew 9:1-8
4. Matthew 15:29-31
(Is Jesus God? He
   predicted His own
   death and
   resurrection.)
5. Mark 10:32-34
6. Matthew 16:15-20
7. Matthew 16:21-23

Jesus Rose from the   Romans 1:4a
   Dead:
1. Luke 18:31-33
2. John 20:1-21
3. Acts 3:15
4. Romans 6:9,10
5. Romans 1:4
6. 1 Corinthians 15:3-8
7. 1 Corinthians 15:20

---

1. Luke 24:36-43   1 Corinthians 3:16
2. Ephesians 1:19,20

The Holy Spirit
3. 1 Corinthians 3:16
4. Matthew 3:13-17
5. Matthew 4:1-4
6. Luke 11:13
7. 2 Corinthians 3:18

15 Months of Nightly Readings

Scripture Reading	*Memory Verse*
1. Romans 15:13	2 Corinthians 3:18
2. 1 John 2:27-29	
3. 2 Peter 1:20,21	
4. Ephesians 4:30-32	
5. John 14:15-27	
6. 1 Corinthians 2:7-16	
7. 1 Corinthians 12:1-7	

1. 2 Corinthians 1:21,22	Romans 8:11
2. Romans 8:4-10	
3. Romans 8:11-17	
4. Galatians 5:16-26	
5. Acts 9:31	
6. John 16:9-14	
7. Luke 2:25-31	

1. Luke 4:1-15	Ephesians 5:18b
2. Luke 4:16-21	
3. Luke 12:9-12	
4. Ephesians 1:13,14	
5. Acts 2:1-18	
6. Ephesians 5:18	
7. Matthew 10:19,20	

1. Hebrews 3:6	Hebrews 6a
2. James 4:5,6	
3. Mark 13:11	
4. John 4:21-23	
5. 1 Corinthians 12:13	
6. 1 Thessalonians 1:5	
7. 1 Peter 1:2,10,11,12	

15 Months of Nightly Readings

Scripture Reading   *Memory Verse*

Jesus Is Coming Again: James 5:8b
1. Colossians 3:3,4
2. John 14:1-3
   James 5:7-9
3. 1 Peter 1:7
   Philippians 2:14-16
4. Acts 1:10,11
5. 1 Thessalonians
   5:23
   1 Corinthians 1:7-9
6. 1 John 2:28
   Job 19:25
7. Daniel 7:1,9-14

---

1. Jeremiah 23:5,6   Mark 14:62
2. Psalm 50:1-6
3. Zechariah 14:1-11
4. Mark 14:61b,62
5. Philippians 3:20
6. Review 1 Corin-
   thians 1:7-9.
7. Review choice of
   verses above.

When Will the Second   Luke 12:40
   Coming Happen?
1. Matthew 24:14,30,
   31,33,36-46
2. Luke 12:35-40
3. 1 Thessalonians 5:1-6
   Matthew 24:27

15 Months of Nightly Readings

Scripture Reading	*Memory Verse*
4. 2 Thessalonians 2:1-12	
Signs of His Coming:	
5. Matthew 24:3-7	
6. Daniel 12:4	
7. Mark 13:10 Mark 10:32-37	

1. 2 Peter 3:1-8	1 Thessalonians 4:17
2. Luke 17:26-37	
3. 2 Timothy 3:1-8	
How Will the Rapture Happen?	
4. John 14:1-3	
5. 1 Corinthians 15:51-58	
6. 1 Thessalonians 4:15-18	
7. Revelation 1:6,7	

God Speaks to the Young:	Ecclesiastes 11:9
1. Ecclesiastes 11:9,10 12:1-7,13	
2. 1 Timothy 4:1-16	
3. Matthew 18:5	
4. Psalm 34:11-17	
5. Jeremiah 1:4-8	
6. Proverbs 23:16-25	
7. Proverbs 23:31-35	

15 Months of Nightly Readings

Scripture Reading	*Memory Verse*

***Some Good Rules
to Live by:***   Proverbs 3:6
1. Proverbs 4:1-9
2. Proverbs 4:10-22
3. Proverbs 18:1-4
4. Proverbs 19:22-23
5. Proverbs 3:1-12
6. Matthew 26:41
7. Galatians 5:16,17

God Gives Instructions: 2 Timothy 3:16
1. 2 Timothy 3:16
2. 2 Timothy 4:1-4
3. Psalm 119:9-20
4. Proverbs 1:7,8
   2 Samuel 22:31
5. James 1:21-25
6. 1 John 2:27,28
7. John 14:15-17
   John 16:12-14

***Knowing Right From
Wrong***   Psalm 25:4
1. James 1:5-9
2. Proverbs 2:1-10
3. Galatians 5:16,25
4. Psalm 25:4-9
   Proverbs 19:27
5. 1 Corinthians
   6:11-13
6. Romans 14:23
7. Romans 15:1-3

15 Months of Nightly Readings

Scripture Reading	Memory Verse
1. Mark 7:20-23	Deuteronomy 6:5,6
2. Proverbs 11:1-17	
3. Deuteronomy 5:5b-21	
4. Deuteronomy 6:1-9,17,18	
5. Isaiah 55:8,9	
6. Proverbs 16:1-9,33	
7. James 1:5	

Scripture Reading	Memory Verse
1. Matthew 7:7-11	Psalm 18:33,36
2. Psalm 48:14	
3. Psalm 73:23,24	
4. Psalm 32:8	
5. Psalm 18:33,36	
6. Isaiah 58:11	
7. Psalm 37:23,24	

Scripture Reading	Memory Verse
1. Psalm 25:4-15 Psalm 119:8 Jeremiah 29:11-13	Micah 6:8
2. Micah 6:7,8	
3. 1 John 4:7,21	
How Should Kids Treat Their Parents?	
4. Proverbs 6:20-23	
5. Proverbs 15:5 Proverbs 13:1 Proverbs 19:26	
6. Proverbs 20:20 Proverbs 23:22 Proverbs 30:17	

15 Months of Nightly Readings

Scripture Reading   *Memory Verse*

7. Proverbs 28:24
   Proverbs 13:13
   Colossians 3:20

---

1. Ephesians 6:1-3   Colossians 3:20
   Exodus 21:15,17
2. Deuteronomy 27:16
3. Matthew 15:1-9
4. Proverbs 30:1-14
5. 1 Timothy 5:1-4
6. Leviticus 20:6-9
7. Colossians 3:20

If You Have Done   1 John 1:9
  Something Wrong:
1. Ecclesiastes 7:20
   1 John 1:9
   Romans 3:23
2. John 5:24
3. Colossians 1:13,14,
   20-23
4. Ephesians 1:4-7
5. Psalm 103:1-12
6. 1 Corinthians 1:8,9
7. Colossians 2:13,14,15

---

1. 2 Corinthians 5:17-21   Acts 13:38b,39
2. Romans 8:29-34
Forgiveness:
3. Romans 4:21-27

15 Months of Nightly Readings

Scripture Reading	*Memory Verse*

4. Acts 13:38,39
5. 1 John 1:8-10
6. Psalm 32:1-6
Jesus Forgave Others:
7. Luke 23:32-34

---

1. John 8:1-11	Psalm 86:5

2. Luke 15:11-24
*David's Prayers for
  Forgiveness:*
3. Psalm 86:5
  Psalm 130:1-5
4. Psalm 51:1-13
5. Romans 3:21,22
6. Psalm 34:17-19
7. Psalm 139:23,24

The Tongue:	Matthew 12:35

1. Proverbs 10:14-19
  Proverbs 11:13
2. Proverbs 13:3
  Proverbs 15:26,28
3. Proverbs 18:6-8,21
4. Proverbs 26:20-22
5. Matthew 12:35-37
6. Matthew 15:16-20
7. Psalm 15:1-5

---

1. Psalm 101:3-5	1 Peter 3:11

2. Psalm 141:2-4

15 Months of Nightly Readings

Scripture Reading　　　　　　*Memory Verse*

3. Jude 14-16
4. 1 Peter 3:10-12
5. James 3:1-12
   Isaiah 50:1-7
   (the way out)
Overeating:
6. 1 Corinthians 6:12,13
7. Proverbs 13:25
   Proverbs 23:19,20

---

1. Proverbs 25:16　　　　Philippians 2:13
2. 2 Peter 2:9
   (There is help.)
   Philippians 2:13
3. Philippians 4:13
   (there is help)
Criticism and Correction:
4. Proverbs 10:17
   Proverbs 12:15
   Proverbs 13:18
5. Proverbs 15:31,32
   Proverbs 19:20
   Proverbs 23:12
6. Proverbs 25:11,12
   Proverbs 28:12,13
7. Proverbs 28:12,13
   (repeat)

How to Treat Our Bodies:　1 Corinthians 3:17
1. Romans 12:1
2. 1 Corinthians 6:19,20

15 Months of Nightly Readings

Scripture Reading	*Memory Verse*

3. 1 Peter 4:1-5
4. Proverbs 23:29-35
5. Proverbs 20:1
   Proverbs 31:4-7
6. Isaiah 5:11-25
7. 1 Samuel 30:16-20

---

1. 1 Timothy 5:22,23   Ephesians 4:32
2. Ephesians 5:18
   2 Peter 1:3,4
Arguing and Quarreling:
3. Philippians 2:14,15
4. 1 Timothy 4:7,8
5. Ephesians 4:31,32
6. James 1:19,20
7. James 4:1-3

---

1. Proverbs 11:12   Proverbs 15:1
   Proverbs 13:9,10
2. Proverbs 15:1
   Proverbs 18:1-3
   Proverbs 30:33
3. Proverbs 12:16,17
   Colossians 3:8
4. Proverbs 13:3
   Proverbs 14:17,29
5. Proverbs 16:24,32
   Proverbs 19:19
6. Proverbs 29:20-23
   Proverbs 22:24,25
Swearing:
7. Exodus 20:7

15 Months of Nightly Readings

Scripture Reading	*Memory Verse*
1. Ephesians 5:3,4,6	Colossians 3:8,10

1. Ephesians 5:3,4,6
2. Matthew 12:33-37
3. Ephesians 4:29
   Luke 6:45
4. Proverbs 10:11
   Matthew 5:13,33-37
5. Colossians 3:8,10
6. Jude 24,25

Stealing:
7. Ephesians 4:28
   Isaiah 61:8

---

1. Proverbs 12:12   Psalm 32:6
   Proverbs 20:10
2. Psalm 101:1-4
   Psalm 32:1-9

Lying:
3. Ephesians 4:23-25
4. Proverbs 6:12-19
5. Proverbs 12:13,14,
   19,20
6. Proverbs 13:5
   Proverbs 25:18
7. Proverbs 26:18,19

---

*What About Going   Exodus 20:11
to Church?*
1. Acts 2:41-47
2. Luke 6:5,6 (Jesus at-
   tended worship
   services.)

15 Months of Nightly Readings

Scripture Reading　　　　　*Memory Verse*

3. Hebrews 10:24,25
4. Acts 20:7
   Acts 13:14
5. Exodus 20:8,11
Money
6. Hebrews 10:34
7. Psalm 40:17
   Proverbs 10:22
   Psalm 102:17

---

1. Psalm 109:30,31　　　　　Matthew 6:34
   Psalm 69:29-33
2. Matthew 7:7-11
3. Matthew 6:25-34
4. 1 Corinthians 3:21-23
5. Proverbs 28:3
   Philippians 3:7-9
6. Proverbs 15:6
   Psalm 111:1-5
7. Psalm 37:16
   James 2:5
   James 1:9

---

1. Luke 6:17-25　　　　　Galatians 4:7
2. 1 Timothy 6:6-10
3. Proverbs 23:4,5
4. Psalm 112:1-3
5. Galatians 4:7
6. Proverbs 8:1-10
7. Proverbs 8:11-21

15 Months of Nightly Readings

Scripture Reading	*Memory Verse*
1. Proverbs 27:24 Proverbs 11:24-28	Psalm 34:10b
2. Matthew 6:31-33	
3. Psalm 34:9-11	
4. Ecclesiastes 5:10-12	
5. Isaiah 58:10,11	
6. Malachi 3:10 Colossians 3:1-4	
7. Proverbs 3:13-18	

How Great God Is:	Jeremiah 32:27
1. Isaiah 40:12-27	
2. Proverbs 8:22-25	
3. Job 28:25,26	
4. Job 37:1-13	
5. Colossians 1:16,17	
6. Jeremiah 32:27	
7. Isaiah 48:12,13 Isaiah 64:8	

	Habakkuk 2:20
1. 1 Chronicles 29:10b-13	
2. Colossians 2:3 Romans 11:33-36	
3. Isaiah 43:10-13 Isaiah 66:1,2	
4. Colossians 1:15-17	
5. Ephesians 3:20 Isaiah 2:19-22	
6. Jeremiah 16:20,21	
7. Jeremiah 17:9,10 Habakkuk 2:20	

15 Months of Nightly Readings

Scripture Reading	*Memory Verse*
1. 2 Chronicles 16:9	Acts 17:24
2. Psalm 107:23-43	
3. Acts 17:24-27	
4. Amos 4:13	
Amos 5:8,9	
5. Proverbs 30:4	
6. Psalm 104:1-17	
7. Psalm 104:18-35	

1. Nahum 1:2-8	Psalm 90:2
2. Psalm 90:1-4	
3. Mark 4:35-41	
4. Habakkuk 3:3-6	
5. Psalm 139:15-18	
6. Isaiah 64:1-4	
7. Isaiah 40:10-26	

How Much Does God Love Us?	John 3:16
1. John 3:16	
2. Romans 3:23	
3. Romans 8:35-39	
4. Ephesians 1:4,5	
5. Ephesians 3:17-19	
6. John 15:9-13	
7. 1 John 3:1	
1 Corinthians 2:9